In this deeply personal book, Deacon Bob Hartman delves into aspects of contemporary human life where we often fear treading, from restlessness and guilt to regret and loneliness. With warmth, insight, and honesty, he shows how these disruptive experiences are actually opportunities for maturing in practices of prayer and reflection that draw us ever more closely into the steady and reassuring presence of God's unconditional love. It is an inspiring and distinctively Christian message of hope and perseverance for life's journey.

—**Richard Corneil, CEO, St. Joseph's Health Care Society**

AMIDST LIFE'S

Clouds,

A NEW DAY!

Encountering the Presence of God

Deacon Bob Hartman

AMIDST LIFE'S CLOUDS, A NEW DAY
Copyright © 2023 by Deacon Bob Hartman

Scripture marked ASV taken from the American Standard Version, which is in the public domain. • Scripture marked CEB taken from the Common English Bible, Copyright © 2011 by Common English Bible. • Scripture marked DRA taken from the Douay-Rheims 1899 American Edition, which is in the public domain. • Scripture marked ERV taken from the Easy-to-Read Version, Copyright © 2006 by Bible League International. • Scripture marked GNT taken from the Good News Translation® (Today's English Version, Second Edition), Copyright © 1992 by American Bible Society. • Scripture marked ISV taken from the International Standard Version, Copyright © 1995–2014 by ISV Foundation. All rights reserved internationally. Used by permission of Davidson Press, LLC. • Scripture marked NABRE taken from the New American Bible (Revised Edition), © 2010, 1991, 1986, 1970 Confraternity of Christian Doctrine, Inc., Washington, DC. All Rights Reserved. • Scripture marked NASB taken from the New American Standard Bible, Copyright © 1960, 1971, 1977, 1995, 2020 by The Lockman Foundation. • Scripture marked NCB taken from the New Catholic Bible, Copyright © 2019 by Catholic Book Publishing Corp. All rights reserved. • Scripture marked NET taken from the New English Translation, NET Bible®, Copyright ©1996-2017 by Biblical Studies Press, L.L.C. http://netbible.com All rights reserved. • Scripture marked NIV taken from The Holy Bible, New International Version®, NIV® Copyright ©1973, 1978, 1984, 2011 by Biblica, Inc.® Used by permission. All rights reserved worldwide. • Scripture marked NKJV taken from the New King James Version®, Copyright © 1982 by Thomas Nelson, Inc. Used by permission. All rights reserved. • Scripture marked NLT taken from the Holy Bible, New Living Translation, Copyright ©1996, 2004, 2015 by Tyndale House Foundation. Used by permission of Tyndale House Publishers, Inc., Carol Stream, Illinois 60188. All rights reserved. • Scripture marked NRSVA taken from New Revised Standard Version Bible: Anglicised Edition, copyright © 1989, 1995 the Division of Christian Education of the National Council of the Churches of Christ in the United States of America. Used by permission. All rights reserved. • Scripture marked RSVCE taken from the Revised Standard Version of the Bible: Catholic Edition, copyright © 1965, 1966 the Division of Christian Education of the National Council of the Churches of Christ in the United States of America. Used by permission. All rights reserved. • Scripture marked VOICE taken from The Voice Bible, Copyright © 2012 Thomas Nelson, Inc. The Voice™ translation © 2012 Ecclesia Bible Society All rights reserved. • Scripture marked WEB taken from the World English Bible, which is in the public domain. The name "World English Bible" is trademarked.

ISBN: 978-1-4866-2415-7
eBook ISBN: 978-1-4866-2416-4

Word Alive Press
119 De Baets Street Winnipeg, MB R2J 3R9
www.wordalivepress.ca

WORD ALIVE
—P R E S S—

Cataloguing in Publication information can be obtained from Library and Archives Canada.

Contents

Our Ultimate Source

Moving Forward

Life Struggles: A Test of Faith or an Invitation to Encounter the Presence of God

Introduction

IN APRIL 2010, my wife Joanne and I attended a presentation on mental illness, sponsored by the Social Justice Committee of St. Michael's Catholic Church here in our hometown of London, Ontario.

The speaker was an advocate for those who suffer from mental illness, and he shared his own story of courage and faith, as one who has come through to the bright and productive side of recovery from the devastation of schizophrenia.

At the conclusion of this presentation, anyone in attendance who had an interest and desire to learn more, and perhaps to get involved in some effort to diminish the stigma of mental illness, was invited to make themselves known.

From this invitation, five individuals eventually met. Over a period of time that involved reading, discussion, and prayer, a decision was made to begin a faith-based outreach to those suffering from mental illness, as well as to family members and friends who support them.

In September 2010, You Are Not Alone (Y.A.N.A.) was formed, from which New Day evolved about one year later. New Day's focus is specifically on those suffering from mental health challenges, while Y.A.N.A. works with those offering very crucial support.

Both groups were modelled on "Welcomed and Valued,"[1] a multi-faith organization backed by the US Catholic Bishops, who in 1978 formed

---

[1] National Catholic Partnership on Disability https://ncpd.org

the National Catholic Partnership on Disability. We are grateful for their kind permission to use and adapt their material to our purposes.

After working with New Day for nearly ten years, I have personally witnessed the power that faith can have in the sometimes long, lonely, uphill journey toward recovery.

What I have learned is that the principles and context practiced by Y.A.N.A. and New Day are beneficial tools that can be applied to daily life for everyone, regardless of mental, physical, or even spiritual health.

Our life journeys can be difficult and confusing. We may have many days when we experience wonder, joy, and great satisfaction in what we do and with those with whom we associate. We also face days when, for whatever reason, we carry disappointments, anxieties, frustrations, loneliness, and challenges.

We are all wounded, scarred, or broken in one way or other. Perhaps we've experienced great hurts: physical, sexual, or emotional abuse; the loss of health or loss of a loved one; separation from a spouse or family member(s); subtle innuendoes; or those more obvious and abrupt occasions that play havoc with our self-confidence and add to our loneliness.

No matter who we are or where we are in our life journey, in our brokenness we all have the need to be welcomed and valued. We are all born with a deep and lasting thirst to feel cared for and loved, and to be given all that we need to grow and flourish in life. I believe from the very depths of my soul that this thirst is a natural and innate desire woven into the fabric of our being by a God of love, a God of compassion, and a God of mercy—a God who wants and calls us to know Him, to love Him, and to welcome Him into our lives every day.

We may not realize or want to acknowledge that every day of our life journey gives us an opportunity toward seeing and hearing God, coming to know to some degree that God is present and alive in our daily lives.

Every day we may be presented with a broad gamut of ups and downs: happiness and joy, struggle and challenge. This has always been part of the history of humankind. Adam and Eve knew the supreme wonder and beauty of creation—the Garden of Eden, with everything they could ever want—yet they were soon enticed to go for the one thing they were told to not partake in, and they gave in to the pressure.

Life has its way of providing teachable moments that demand patience, acceptance, and perseverance. Perhaps the greatest lesson we are offered—though very often it's one we tend to resist—is coming to terms with the fact we cannot manage it all on our own, that we need to trust and rely on God to direct and guide us through the course.

What follows is a glimpse at my journey and my struggles, as I come to recognize more fully, one day at a time, God's presence in my life, and in doing so, come to a clearer, keener awareness of who I am, where I come from, and where I am called to be.

A friend recently introduced me to the writings of Josephine Lombardi, who says it so clearly and succinctly: "Your future depends on you knowing God and knowing yourself. This will bring you healing, and your own story of healing will inspire others to know God and to know themselves."[2]

This is my desire for you. This is my hope in sharing what I see as personal encounters with God in the course of daily life, encounters that can bring purpose and meaning in life.

I have chosen to use the format that was used with success in the New Day outreach: a brief text to help us recognize how we are doing and what we are experiencing on a feeling level, followed by a passage from Sacred Scripture to help us relate our experience and/or feeling to our faith. Each chapter entails a brief thought or reflection on what may be learned to help give us encouragement and hope, and perhaps even lead us toward a new outlook—a *New Day*.

I begin by acknowledging and thanking my dear wife, who has stood by me for over five decades with love, support, acceptance, and forgiveness. She has shared with me her strong and steady faith, and in doing so has strengthened that wonderful gift of faith within me.

---

[2] Josephine Lombardi, *Experts in Humanity: A Journey of Self-Discovery and Healing* (Novalis, 2016), p. 127.

Dedication

NO MATTER WHO we are or what we have done or may do in life, we don't get there on our own. There is always someone else who has given us the inspiration, the desire, the determination, and the confidence to move forward and do it. Someone who has loved us and made us feel worthy of being loved and loving.

It is in love that we are empowered to do what God calls us to do, and it is in and through others that we experience not only the love of another, but the love of God Himself.

It is through God's love and compassion that we come to know ourselves as individuals.

The reality is that many people influence us, from childhood right to the end of life. Some people influence us in a positive way, and some in a negative way. Either way, groundwork is laid as to how we mature, think, act, perceive, love, and accept ourselves and others—or how we fail to do those things.

Here, at the beginning of this book, I introduce you to my wife Joanne, the joy and love of my life.

Joanne has experienced many hardships. She has suffered many waves of abuse, and still deals with the aftermath: post-traumatic stress and other residual remains. Every day seems to be a fight for her to find enjoyment and prolonged peace.

Yet, through it all, she holds tight to her faith and trusts in the love, mercy, and compassion of God. She goes to Mary, our Blessed Mother, for guidance and help in bringing her fears and needs directly to her son Jesus.

Through it all, she is always present to others in need: to me, to our children, grandchildren, friends, and strangers alike. She holds many people in her heart, praying that they recognize and accept God's love and direction for their lives.

I have been a retired deacon for over four years now. During this time, I have been greatly blessed in being here for and with Joanne. I have learned from her, in a very direct way, what is involved in perseverance, what it is to feel depleted of abilities that used to be taken for granted, how to endure things that are not wanted, and most of all, what it means to surrender it all to God—not always without a fight.

I am also learning that the greatest gift I can give her is my presence. Sometimes that entails helping to do things around the house. Sometimes it takes the form of talking, sharing, and accepting our feelings. Sometimes it means being humble enough to admit that I have no magic answer, but that I can be still and quiet in a way that honours her and gives her comfort.

Every day, morning and evening, we pray together the Liturgy of the Hours. Every day we pray the rosary together. We try to attend Mass as often as we can, even if it has to be via social media.

We take time to reflect on who God is in our lives and in our marriage, and who we are to God. I have grown in faith over this time as I've sat next to Joanne in the pew at Mass, after ten years of her sitting by herself while I served at God's table.

I am learning that God's table is indeed everywhere and anywhere, wherever and whenever we invite Him to be with us. I am precisely where I am called to be in serving God as a deacon.

There are times of discouragement for both of us, but this is a time in which I am discovering precisely why I was ordained a permanent deacon: namely, so I can recognize every gift of the Holy Spirit in my life, and to do my utmost to live out those gifts in service with and for others, beginning right here at home with Joanne.

With God's ongoing grace, I look forward to welcoming each new day that I am given. I welcome my Lord into my day, to lead me, to teach me, and to grow me into whom He created me to be.

Through Joanne, I am better able to recognize God's very presence in life.

Through her, God's constant, steady love for me has become so very tangible and personal.

Through Joanne, God's compassion, mercy, and forgiveness continue to be revealed to me in very personal and intimate ways. That is the grace and fruit that flows through the sacrament of our marriage.

Every day I give thanks for all I have been given, especially for the gift of love given to me in the person of Joanne.

I love you, my dear, and I thank you for being you, for loving me as I am, and for helping me become more.

Welcomed and Valued

EVERYONE COMES INTO this world, to life, as a small fragile infant, totally dependent on someone else to provide everything we need to survive, grow, and come into our own. And who we become reflects, to some degree, where we came from and how we were raised. The values and morals that were or were not instilled in us, the self-confidence and sense of self-worth that we were either given or denied, the expectations and tone in which we were spoken to as children—basically all that we experienced in our early years of development: all of these things shape and form who we become as adults, and how we cope and deal with the inevitable struggles of daily life.

That is not to say that all our troubles and anxieties in life stem from our upbringing. No, we have to take responsibility for how we live our adult lives. We make plenty of mistakes on our own that put us in uncomfortable and regrettable situations.

Whether we carry baggage from our youth or baggage from our choices as adults, many of us struggle in dealing with who we are. Maybe we are in a daily fight with anxiety, depression, or one of the many other challenges to our mental well-being. Perhaps we are experiencing ill health, or the deep sadness that comes with the loss of someone we love. Or we may be feeling a sense of failure as a spouse or parent, or in a business or work environment. Any one of these experiences can do a number on our psyche, and we will explore more as we progress through these pages.

We can easily become disappointed, discouraged, and embittered, not only with ourselves but toward those we are in contact with. Our self-worth might sink to new lows, and we may lose our sense of purpose and meaning.

It has been said that the single greatest illness of the twenty-first century is loneliness, and it is widespread through all levels of society. Loneliness is a modern-day pandemic.

Indeed, we must acknowledge the bad things we experience—our mistakes and our misfortunes—if we hope to move beyond them.

It takes time and courage to face our brokenness, but in doing so we can begin to realize that there is far more to us than what we do, or the stuff we encounter and have to deal with throughout our life journey.

In the first book of Sacred Scripture, we read that we are created in the very image and likeness of God (Genesis 1:27).

Canadian psychologist Dr. David G. Benner writes:

Wholeness in Humanity, spare me perfection. Give me instead the wholeness that comes from embracing the full reality of who I am, just as I am. Paradoxically, it is this whole self that is most perfect.

As it turns out, wholeness, not perfection, is the route to the actualization of our deepest humanity. Inconsistencies, imperfections, and failures to live up to ideals are all part of what it means to be human.

What seems to distinguish those who are most deeply and wholly human is not their perfection, but their courage in accepting their imperfections. Accepting themselves as they are, they then become able to accept others as they are.[3]

Our lives are in balance when our Body, our Mind, our Spirit, and our Relationships with others are in order. Our purpose in our personal lives, in the life of the Church and the life of our communities, grows and enriches as we recognize and accept God's presence in our everyday life—recognizing that we are indeed loved and valued by the One who created us, who sustains us and who welcomes us into newness every *New Day* with Him.

---

[3] David G. Benner, "Perfection and the Harmonics of Wholeness," "Perfection," *Oneing,* Vol. 4, No. 1 (CAC: 2016), 61-63.

Thought for Reflection:

How well do I accept my weaknesses and my imperfections?

Do I perhaps lack the courage to do so?

How readily am I able to accept the mistakes and imperfections of others?

> ...the Lord who created you says,
>> "Do not be afraid—I will save you.
>>> I have called you by name—you are mine.
>>> When you pass through deep waters, I will be with you;
>>> your troubles will not overwhelm you. (Isaiah 43:1–2, GNT)

Thought for Reflection:

In what area do I need to focus at this time to bring balance to my life?

When have I truly felt that I was God's—that He knows me and loves me?

A Look Within

One
A Look at Who We Are

AS WE BEGIN to think critically about our lives, very often it is the chaos of daily existence that first comes to mind. Our lives are busy, and our lives are fast.

As children, there simply are not enough hours in the day to do what we want—to play and discover the many mysteries of life and creation.

As we grow a little older, there doesn't seem to be adequate time to develop a deep appreciation for all that we have discovered. There's always something more that is new and intriguing.

As young adults, our lives are busy as we further our education and try to find employment that allows us to exercise our skills, dreams, and hopes. At this point, life is more focused on the future than on the present.

I know as a young adult I was very intent and eager to establish myself: to be a conscientious contributor to society, a caring and loving husband, a nurturing father, and a faithful Christian. But the reality was that I hadn't yet come to truly know myself. How could I possibly know how to do what life was calling me to do?

I was blessed as a very young adult to fall in love with Joanne, an amazing equally young woman. We were married on June 8, 1968, when we were in our early twenties. Fifty-five years later, we are still learning, with each other's help, who we are, and our meaning and purpose in life.

We have also learned that love is far more than attraction. Love is challenging one another to be the very best we can be, to be as fully as humanly possible whom God created us to be. I am a richer, happy man through Joanne's love, and every day I thank God for the gift of her in my life.

Three days before our first anniversary, Joanne and I were blessed with our first son, followed by a daughter and then another son in short order. Very quickly we discovered that our daily routine took on new twists and new challenges.

Parenthood has a way of bringing us to a more intense focus on who we are as individuals, who we are as a couple, and what we want to offer our children.

Inevitably there came the challenge of dealing with sickness, then the bouts of asthma, and the first time one of our own had to be admitted to a hospital.

Our children became our focus, and they remained so throughout their childhood, their teens, and well into their adulthood. Now we think about and worry about their jobs, their health, and their children.

Then came the day we'd worked all our life for: finally, it was time to retire and take life easy. For some, this is a huge decision and an even greater adjustment. For me, let's just say that my career was a job, and I looked forward to the day when I could walk away.

Life is busy, and if and when there is a quiet lull, we quickly find something to fill the gap. Oh, how we struggle with inactivity and quietness.

Two years before my retirement, I entered into formation and development studies at St. Peter's Seminary in London. Four years later, I was ordained a permanent deacon for the Diocese of London.

This was an incredible journey of deep discovery of who I am, and who God is calling me to be. How could I possibly serve Him and His people? To be honest, I worked hard to get through grade twelve. I had a very hard time reading and comprehending things.

I remember a teacher telling me in grade ten to get out of any history and geography studies as soon as I possibly could. The prospect of serving God as an ordained member of the clergy was initially somewhat terrifying.

Truth be told, the call to ministry was a few years in the making. It was a call that I kept denying until finally, Joanne said, why not find out what it's all about and take it from there? And so began my journey of learning, spiritual growth, and development. By the time I was ordained, God had reassured me of many things, but the following three are the clearest in my mind.

> *Do not fear, for I* have *redeemed you;* I have called you *by your name;* you *are Mine!* (Isaiah 43:1, NASB, emphasis added)

> You have *not* chosen *me: but* I have chosen you*; and have appointed* you*, that* you *should go, and should bring forth fruit.* (John 15:16, DRA, emphasis added)

> *The Holy Spirit will* give you *the* words *to say at the moment when* you *need them.* (Luke 12:12, VOICE)

Life truly is a journey, and as in any journey, we will have to maneuver through many twists, turns, and detours. We will face smooth patches as well as rough terrain, and undoubtedly have to go over many roads under construction.

Most importantly, our journey can be enriched through a vast array of discoveries about life, our roles, and our responsibilities, both as individuals and as a community. There are many roads to travel, and there is much searching to do, but the greatest discovery will come to fruition through our acceptance of God's invitation to share life with Him, to deepen our relationships with Him and with one another as we move step-by-step toward our ultimate destination with one discovery after another, one *New Day* after another.

Thought for Reflection:

What is God asking me to do for Him today?

Do I believe and trust that God will provide everything I need to listen to what He asks of me, and to follow through in doing His will?

Two

Doubting *Who?*

Unless I see the mark of the nails in his hands, and put my finger in the mark of the nails and my hand in his side, I will not believe. (John 20:25, NRSVA)

THIS IS THE background, the scene, in which "the apostle Thomas personally experiences the mercy of God, which has a concrete face, the face of Jesus. Thomas does not believe it when the other apostles tell him, 'We have seen the Lord.' It isn't enough for him that Jesus had foretold it, promised it: 'On the third day I will rise.' He wants to see; he wants to put his hand in the place of the nails and in Jesus' side."[4]

This is one week before Jesus appears to his apostles for the second time in the upper room. This time Thomas is there, along with the other apostles. Jesus gave Thomas time to reflect on what the others had told him about what had happened the prior week. Jesus was well aware of Thomas's doubt. I imagine that was surely part of the reason why he came back to the upper room that second time when Thomas was there. When someone hurts us by having no belief, trust, or faith in us, we may be inclined to shun them, but Jesus is different. He is not harsh or rash with Thomas for his questioning or

---

[4] From Pope Francis's homily on Divine Mercy Sunday, 2013. https://www.vatican.va/content/francesco/en/ homilies/2013/documents/pappa-francesco 220130407 ome-lia-possesso-cattedra-laterano.html

his doubting; rather, He offers His understanding. He greets Thomas and the others with compassion, mercy, and peace. He greets us in the very same way.

"Peace be with you" is much more than simply a warm welcome. "Peace be with you" is a call to reflection.

True peace comes to me through reflecting on and acknowledging just who I am—with all my strengths and all my weaknesses, what I have done and what I have failed to do—in terms of whom God created me to be and to do, with a deep recognition and appreciation of Jesus' presence in my life and God's unconditional love for me despite my many failings.

Often I doubt God and ask the question: Why does He continue to love me and offer me peace? But no matter how many times I do so, His presence and His peace are undoubtable in my life and the lives of those around me, in our faith communities, and in the world. Jesus continually says to every single person: *"Peace be with you."*

Every moment of our day, from beginning to end, is filled with many things, sometimes to the point of overflowing. Whether we are alone or in the company of others, there are realities of life that we process in both mind and heart. We often choose to go through some of them on our own. We may be celebrating a personal accomplishment in utter silence, or quietly with a trusted friend. We may be in a state of anger or grief or anguish over something that has happened and we are not yet ready or able to share with anyone else.

Other realities come to our attention through our interactions and our relationships with others. Those too may be joyful and celebratory in nature, or they may be difficult, disturbing encounters that rattle our trust, overturn our confidence, and cause us to question our faith. "Life stuff" can raise us up or it can shake us to the core.

Hopefully, we have many moments when we experience quiet, rest, relaxation, rejuvenation, and peace. But those other moments of unrest, disquiet, turmoil, and anxieties? They too are part of the fabric of everyday life.

There are many times in my day when I find myself asking: what in the world is all of this about? Why now?

The far better and more important question for me to ask myself would be: what it is that I am supposed to learn from this? What is God trying to help me be aware of, to change, to do something about? Who is it that God wants me to be thinking about and praying for?

Every day we are given multiple opportunities to meet and encounter Jesus, whether it be through others, or in the silence of our hearts. But I think we have to be willing and wanting to experience these encounters, to open our eyes to experience a true, deep, real, face-to-face meeting with Christ in every one of these opportunities.

Put your finger here and see my hands. Reach out your hand and put it in my side. Do not doubt but believe. (John 20:27, NRSVA)

This was Jesus's invitation to Thomas, who expressed doubt that Jesus had been seen alive. It was also His invitation to Peter, who had denied even knowing Him when things got tough and dangerous. It was Jesus's invitation to the rest of His apostles, except one, who walked away from him and hid. And it is Jesus's invitation to you and to me to meet Him, to know Him personally, to have an intimate relationship with Him.

I don't know about you, but there are times when I question God's presence in my life. It isn't easy to have perfect, complete, and constant trust and faith. We can't do it, let alone sustain it on our own. Faith and trust in God are God's gift. It is God who shows us how, who invites us to see, touch, and recognize Him.

He reveals himself to us so that we might come to believe, that we might profess our faith in Him and attest that He is very much alive and present to us. Jesus invited and led Thomas to believe in His presence, and He does so with us. Our ever-loving God longs to hear our questions and doubts. In raising questions about faith and trust in God, we open ourselves to receive answers. God longs to hear us speak to Him with honesty. In expressing our frustration—even our anger and doubts—we open that void within us for God to fill, to satisfy.

God longs to see our trust and reliance on Him, and He longs to hear us profess our faith in the risen Lord, just as Thomas did: *"My Lord and my God!"* (John 20:28, NIV).

Surely it was a simple matter for Thomas to declare Jesus as Lord and God. After all, he knew it was Jesus standing in front of him, and he could see the wounds, the nail marks, and the hole where the sword had pierced His side. Jesus even invited him to feel, to put his hand in the hole. Thomas could no longer deny what he saw with his own eyes.

We might think Thomas was lucky, that he saw the proof he needed. There is a bit of Thomas in all of us. We simply cannot comprehend this mystery of God's love. Very often, we too want to see. Individually we question: could He really love me that much? Perhaps the answer to that question lies in our faith, in our belief in what has been handed down to us, of what we have learned and witnessed, and above all our belief in our Baptismal promises.

We have all seen the signs we need to believe and to say for ourselves, "My Lord and my God."

In the Eucharist, the sacred sacrifice of Mass, Jesus Himself comes before us at the table of the Word, and at the table of the Lord. When the priest raises the host, he says in the very person of Jesus the words of consecration: "This is My Body." Then he raises the chalice of wine and says, "This is My Blood."

This is the pinnacle of our belief, the source and summit of our faith. This is the perfect time to raise our eyes, to recognize Christ and to gaze upon His risen Body and His Blood and let our hearts cry out in joy, "My Lord and my God!"

And when we receive Jesus in Holy Communion, once again we declare him as Lord and God. Amen, so it is.

Eucharist is a communal celebration where people of faith gather together as the body of Christ, as the Church, in prayer and in worship to give glory, praise, and thanks to God for offering his Son to give us forgiveness, and for opening up for us the way to our eternal home as Daughters and Sons of God, for the beauty of creation and for life itself. As one single body of Christ, we ask for God's help and guidance so that we may grow in our knowledge and love of God and of one another, as we listen to His Word, proclaimed aloud and whispered in our hearts. As a Church, we offer intercessory prayers for ourselves, for those we love, for our communities, and for the world.

To utter the words "My Lord and my God" with conviction is far more than a prayer. "My Lord and my God" expresses a deep realization of being loved—not in some general sense, but in a very personal and intimate manner. It expresses a mutual relationship with our risen Savior.

When I say "My Lord and my God," I am acknowledging Jesus for who He is, Lord and God. At the same time, I am accepting Jesus as *my* Lord and *my* God. I am inviting Him into my heart, into every aspect of my life, in the very same way that He invites me into a relationship with Him.

This is a relationship expressed throughout scripture, beginning in Genesis 17:7 (NIV): "*I will establish my covenant as an everlasting covenant between me and you and your descendants after you for the generations to come, to be your God and the God of your descendants after you.*"

Prophet after prophet spoke the same truth. Ezekiel and Jeremiah used the same words. And St. Paul preached to the Corinthians: "*For we are the temple of the living God; as God said, 'I will dwell in them and walk among them, and I will be their God, and they shall be my people.'*" (2 Corinthians 6:16, NRSVA).

Like with any of our human relationships, our relationship with Christ is not easy to maintain. We get bombarded with so many opposing messages, and so many temptations draw us away from Him. Sin plays havoc with any relationship, including our relationship with God.

"My Lord and my God" can also be an expression of awe when we gaze upon a crucifix or other image of the crucified Christ. If we reflect on His passion and death, and if we allow ourselves to ponder all the accusations, rejection, beatings, humiliation, pain, and suffering that Jesus accepted and bore for us for our salvation, then we can begin to see the overwhelming awe that is the mystery of God's love.

Reflect too on why He would do such a thing. Consider: people had turned to worshipping idols, the authorities fought Him, many of the religious leaders were pursuing their own agendas, and his own followers abandoned Him when things got tough for them. Yet God in His mighty love redeemed us. That was why He gave us Jesus, His Son, the incarnate, born like you and I were born, to live life with all its marvels and with all its trappings. He did this so that Jesus could show us first-hand how to live a full, meaningful, and fruitful life, and lead us to the Father and our eternal home in the kingdom of God.

Jesus freely chose to give His life for us, out of love for His Father and His love for us, and to carry out the will of his Father: *"Now this is the will of the one who sent me—that I should not lose one person of every one he has given me, but raise them all up at the last day"* (John 6:39, NET). "My Lord and my God," thank You for Your mercy and forgiveness.

I am quite sure that most of us can look back on our lives and readily recall a time, a situation, when we felt lost, helpless, trapped in grief or pain or some turmoil or darkness that we saw no way out of. We may well still feel the weight, carry the bruises, and question what's next. We probably still struggle, but we know that somehow we have gotten through that time, that situation that we thought was out of control, unmanageable, impossible to bear. We know in the very pit of our gut that it is God who walked with us and at times lifted us and carried us. God gives us the grace, the strength, and the patience we need to endure, to face one minute, one day at a time.

What a wonderful relief it is that we do not have to bear the various weights and challenges of life alone—that we truly can rely on You, "My Lord and my God."

As Jesus said to Thomas, *"Have you believed because you have seen me? Blessed are those who have not seen and yet have come to believe"* (John 20:29, NRSVA).

We are those whom Jesus referred to as "those who have not seen and yet have come to believe." And indeed, how blessed we are. Many of us are cradle Catholics, cradle Christians, and for us, it was one or both of our parents, grandparents, a sibling, relative, friend, minister, priest, or religious who passed on and inspired in us what they had come to believe. For other people, faith came more as a definitive moment of conversion, as was the case with Saul.

No matter how we were introduced to the faith, it all began because someone or something planted the seed. The nourishment of that seed is a life-long process. It takes time and effort to nourish that seed so that it may grow and mature. Even Jesus's words *"have come to believe"* insinuate that belief in God is a process—a journey that is the ultimate goal of life. Often it is realized in bits and pieces in hindsight, as I noted earlier.

Remembering when God has been present to us and when He has accompanied us in past struggles and pain gives us hope that God will never abandon us, but will help us in whatever we have yet to face. Faith is not something that we can grasp on our own. It is a gift from God.

Jesus promised to send the Holy Spirit: *"…the Advocate, the Holy Spirit, whom the Father will send in my name, will teach you all things and will remind you of everything I have said to you"* (John 14:26, NIV).

It is the Holy Spirit who leads us to faith, who instills in our hearts that desire, that thirst, that longing to meet and know the risen Lord. We are made members of the Body of Christ through the reception of the sacrament of Baptism. Our faith is fed and nourished through God's grace, through God's Word, through the sacraments, through the strength and movement of the Holy Spirit in us and around us every moment of every day of our lives.

It is significant that this passage, which we often think of as being about "doubting Thomas," occurs the week following Easter Sunday. Post-passion death and resurrection, Jesus is well aware of the denials, of being abandoned by those He had called to follow Him, yet He desires our presence. He desires to shower His love and peace, His unfathomable gifts, on us. He desires to fill our every need. He calls us to follow Him in all that we do, and in all our relationships and interactions with others. He calls us to believe in Him so we may share with others all that He offers, so we may carry out his mission, the will of God—His Father and our Father.

This is the Easter mystery, the mystery of faith, Christ's cry to all humanity: *"O that my people would listen to me, that Israel would walk in my ways! Then I would quickly subdue their enemies, and turn my hand against their foes"* (Psalm 81:13–14, NRSVA).

Thought for Reflection:

In what circumstances do I find myself doubting that God is with me?

How might Thomas's honesty and questioning inspire and perhaps alter the way I pray and talk to God?

What is one instance when I know that God carried me through a hard time? How do I respond to God even now about that instance?

The other disciples told him, "We have seen the Lord!" (John 20:25, NET)

Thought for Reflection:

In what situations or circumstances do I most often see or experience the Lord in my life?

Who is it that most often affirms for me the presence of the Lord?

Three
Tidbits of Light

AS I NOTED in the introduction, every one of us is broken in one way or another. The whole of civilization is broken and always has been—at least ever since the fall of our first parents, Adam and Eve, in the garden of Eden. Ever since that time, humans have had an unwavering need to follow their own agendas. We all seem to have a hard time listening to and following the way God has set out for us.

My life journey seems to have been quite easy when I consider the struggles many people face. I have never been without shelter, clothes, or a place to call home. I have never known the pain of being hungry while being unable to fill that emptiness. But no one gets a pass on hardship, struggle, pain, suffering, loss, doubt, fear, loneliness, or some other feeling of being incomplete. It may be for a brief, fleeting period, but we all face the reality that life here on earth is not perfect. It is often downright difficult.

In a very real manner, our journey here is a training ground, a battlefield where we learn to find our way to our eternal homeland. We have to fight for our inner peace, to learn to give and take from the many lessons life throws our way. This is the place we learn, little by little, what it is to be loved and to love—one day at a time, one step after another.

In my journey thus far, I have experienced incredible happiness and joys, but I also have had moments in life that were times of chaos, times I didn't know where to turn, what to do, or how to do whatever it was that needed to be done. Emptiness can appear in many disguises.

I am the youngest in a family of ten. Born and raised on a farm, I inherited a wonderful awe for the natural beauty that surrounds us. It is there, but we have to take the time to look, observe, listen, and take it all in.

Animal sounds intrigue me. They have their unique way of communicating with each other and with us. Anyone with a pet dog or cat, or I imagine any other pet, recognizes the language of friendship and love when they just want to be near you. They know when we do not feel well, and they offer unconditional comfort.

Each one of us is formed and created as a fragile individual, right from the moment we were conceived. Created fragile and born into a fragile world very much in need, we are dependent from the beginning on much more than ourselves. We are created with a pang of hunger, and a need for others for survival and growth, for friendship and companionship. Long before we are ever able to realize it, we search for someone to model our life after.

We each have much to be grateful for, but I suspect that at some point in life, most of us sense a hollowness within—a void in our lives, a sense that something is missing and there has to be more. Such feelings are not only normal, but important to pay attention to if we are to develop a healthy sense of who we are, what we aspire to, and what we need to reach our potential.

Two and a half months shy of my fifth birthday, my father was killed in a tragic farming accident. He was forty-eight years of age.

The only distinct memory I have of my father is where I sat at the big kitchen table—at the front right corner with Dad at my right at the end of the table, and Mom at my left.

I have a picture of just me and Dad. I am sitting beside him, leaning up against the tire of the tractor. He has his arm around me and a big smile on his face that tells me he loved me. It's a wonderful picture that I treasure, but that is what it is—a picture, with no memory to give it life.

The loss of my dad at such a young age had a tremendous impact on me, as I am sure it did on my mother and siblings.

I never had the experience of knowing who he was as a father, as a husband, and as a Christian man, at least never directly from my immediate family.

I was able to put things together, and learned that my mom had an emotional breakdown after the accident. Maybe that was the reason my siblings never talked about Dad, nor what happened to him. Perhaps they were trying to protect Mom, and thought that talking about him would be too painful for her. So, he was never talked about—almost like he never existed. I had a void that no one was able, or willing, to fill. It was a void that carried on well into my adulthood.

It's a bit unnerving how normal events can bring things forward that have been long tucked away and stored in the back of the mind. For example, when each of our children reached their fifth birthday, that marked a milestone for me. The same thing happened when I passed my forty-eighth year. It was like a part of the history of my life was not going to be repeated in the lives of our children and our family.

When I was well into my fifties, I began to wonder if my dad had taken his own life. When I questioned my family, I was told that was not what happened. Even at that age, I was offered no satisfactory explanation for the silence through all those years. I was told that many of my nephews and nieces knew more about their grandfather than I knew about him—my father. That was not a comforting piece of information for me to hear. It was not a happy occasion.

In my mind, I felt cheated. I wasn't able to experience first-hand the role model that a father should be to his child—a first-hand insight into how a loving husband ought to communicate with the love of his life and with his children, which would offer a glimpse of what real love is all about.

I mentioned earlier that Joanne has been a consistent source of strength and support. She has an unshakable faith in a God who knows only how to love. And as long as I have known her, she has had a great devotion to our Blessed Mother.

Many years ago, we began to pray the rosary together, and the more we did so, the more I began to pay attention—not so much to the words of the prayers, but to Mary's presence as she listened attentively. I began to think of her as truly being my mother, just as Jesus said when He gave her to us through His beloved disciple when He said to his mother, *"here is your son,"* and to the disciple, *"Here is your mother"* (John 19:26–27, NIV).

As I fall in love with Mary more and more, I know she is leading me closer to her son, who can provide those little pieces of light that give me hope, that help me see beyond the moments of loneliness, of anger, of my doubts about my value and worth as a husband, father, and man, and—yes—even of my very real anger toward God for things that have happened. We all need little pieces of light to bring us out of our darkness. Even the darkness that we create through our own thoughts and fears.

It is not unusual for those who have been in deep depression or sorrow for a prolonged period of time to doubt the light's arrival when the first rays begin to lift onto the inner horizon. When light approaches so do hesitation, doubt, confusion, and questions about the light's authenticity. Painful emotions associated with extended despondency have hung on for so long. How could it be that an end has arrived? The pessimistic, weary, beaten down doubtful part of the self tends to respond to the glimpsed light with "Oh, this won't last… I can't afford to believe I might be feeling good again. I don't want to be disappointed… I must be imagining this… Is this really a turning point? Can I be happy again? I've forgotten how that feels. Can I trust it?[5]

Thought for Reflection:

Looking back on my life, can I see what I've learned from a difficult time?

---

[5] Joyce Rupp, *Little Pieces of Light: Darkness and Personal Growth.* Mahwah, NJ: Paulist Press, 2016. E-book. Chapter 5.

Jesus entered Jericho and was passing through. A man was there by the name of Zacchaeus; he was a chief tax collector and was wealthy. He wanted to see who Jesus was, but because he was short he could not see over the crowd. So he ran ahead and climbed a sycamore-fig tree to see him, since Jesus was coming that way.

When Jesus reached the spot, he looked up and said to him, "Zacchaeus, come down immediately. I must stay at your house today." So he came down at once and welcomed him gladly.

All the people saw this and began to mutter, "He has gone to be the guest of a sinner."

But Zacchaeus stood up and said to the Lord, "Look, Lord! Here and now I give half of my possessions to the poor, and if I have cheated anybody out of anything, I will pay back four times the amount."

Jesus said to him, "Today salvation has come to this house, because this man, too, is a son of Abraham. For the Son of Man came to seek and to save the lost." (Luke 19:1–10, NIV)

Thought for Reflection:

Zacchaeus wanted to see Jesus, so he ran ahead of the crowd and climbed a tree. He made a real and great effort to see Jesus, and Jesus saw his desire, his thirst, and his faith.

In this journey of life, many things can disrupt our lives—our body, mind, spirit, and our relationships with others.

Take whatever time you need to recognize and appreciate even the slightest little piece of light that has shone on your life. Take time to reflect on what it might mean to catch a glimpse of Jesus in your presence (even if only in your imagination), and time to allow that wonderment to expand, to grow, to provide hope, and to add reason to look forward to each and every *New Day*.

Four

Having Courage

I THINK IT is pretty safe to say that everyone, at some point in life, gets discouraged. We might get tired of fighting shame or disappointment or anger or fear, or the anxiety that comes when we feel bombarded by negativity. Whether that negativity relates to something within—our behaviour or action—or it comes from outside of ourselves—something we witnessed or experienced, or even some of the things that are happening in today's world—it can wear us down.

We all have done or said things that we regret—things we would prefer no one else ever learns about. And we have all had things done or said to us that have left an undeniable mark—some in a very positive way, for which we are grateful, and others that have been anything but helpful.

Family life and family structure today would be unrecognizable to people living in the past. Seventy-plus years ago when I grew up, men and women seemed willing and determined to endure life and all the struggles that came with it. Faith and belief in God were the cornerstones, not only for the church but for the family. A mere ten years ago, the typical family structure consisted of a man and a woman, a mother and father to any child they were blessed with.

Today, that situation is far different, specifically in our western society where the majority of children are raised by a single parent; for the most part, that appears to be by choice. Many other children have either two mothers or two fathers, and others have a parent or parents who may be bisexual. While these varied family types may be in total opposition to what we may personally believe in, or how we see the role of man and woman as created by God, we must recognize and appreciate the fact that God denies nobody of the need and desire to love and to be loved. He loves every one of His children and wants each one to know and experience love—*His love.*

We also need to recognize and appreciate the fact that children tend to grow up mirroring what they have seen and witnessed throughout their lives.

While every parent has the absolute right and responsibility to raise their children in the way they believe to be best for the child, I think it is unfair to a child, and an outright lie for any parent who does not believe in God or who does not practice their faith, to say they will leave it to their child to make such a decision on their own when they grow up. By that time, their belief in the risen Lord has little chance to flourish without having witnessed a lived expression of faith in the lives of their parents or others who are very close to them.

There is a certain "routine" that a follower of Jesus Christ must establish if he or she is to remain faithful and be fruitful in the faith.

That routine is the very essence of how, firstly, we grow in our faith, and secondly, how we live out our faith.

That routine includes spending quiet time with God every day, reading and listening to His Word, and integrating His Word into our daily life. That "routine" includes opening our hearts and minds to receive Jesus in the Eucharist, and getting to know His Holy Spirit. We first receive the Holy Spirit at baptism, and become strengthened in Him through confirmation and receiving the other sacraments of our faith.

That routine includes the humble admission of our sinfulness and brokenness before God and before others, our repentance for wrong-doings, and a hearty resolve to avoid the scenarios and situations that tempt us to fall once again. It means going to Jesus, seeking His mercy, His forgiveness, and His grace so that we may be strong in our resolve.

That routine includes our conscious desire and effort to love others as God loves us, to show patience and mercy toward others as Christ has been patient and merciful with us. That routine—or the lack of it—is ingrained and set long before a child reaches the age of being able to make serious life decisions.

In recent years, there have been great debates about legislative changes in some of the U.S. states concerning a woman's right to abortion. Regrettably, here in Canada, abortion is legal at all stages of pregnancy. Canada is the only nation that has absolutely no specific restrictions on abortion. Abortion has become something that is perceived by so many as normal, and any attempt to safeguard the unborn is seen as a step back in time regarding a woman's rights over her own body. Whatever happened to the notion that the rights of both women and men over their bodies can and ought to be exercised long before a pregnancy ever comes to be? Both men and women have the right to say "no," and should expect that right to be respected. They have the right to go against peer pressure, to stand firm in what they know and believe to be right and moral, the right to be true to themselves and to honour their being as a child of God.

So many families struggle to stay intact. So many things seem to get in the way of married couples. So many suffer the toll of infidelity and abuse. The challenge of open communication is somehow tightened even further in the presence of social media.

Separation and divorce are common. Disagreements and disputes be-tween family members fester until the rifts become schisms, and relationships cease. Work, sports, and stuff seem to take priority over spending time togeth-er, praying together, laughing together, and enjoying one another's company.

There is a rapid and changing pace of societal norms. No one—young or old, rich or poor—seems to be exempt from the many devastating events that we experience or read about in the news.

Hundreds of thousands of people from all over the world, including here, are displaced by violence, terror, and severe poverty, and seek refuge and safe haven—a place to call home.

Every day we come face to face with violence and fighting, murders, ad-dictions of all kinds, terrorist attacks, abuse in all its ugly variations, and an ever-increasing number of suicides. There appear to be so many people who live in darkness and who have so little expectation or hope of things getting better—of ever being able to have a New Day.

Every generation has had its issues, but today everything that happens is more in our faces. With instant news and social media, we get bombarded with so many things that can bring us down.

That can take our focus and our attention away from our Creator, our God who loves us and desires more than anything else to have a deep and abiding relationship with us.

With faith and deep trust, we need to bring our doubts, our disappointments, our fears and anxieties to God.

We need to pray for His grace to be able to face all that confronts and affronts us daily. We need God's grace and assurance that so long as we have breath, there is a tomorrow, and with His help, we can look forward to and welcome a *New Day* with courage that only God can give and sustain within us.

To live is to change, and to be perfect is to have changed often.[6]

Thought for Reflection:

How do you relate to change?

Is it something you embrace or resist?

---

[6] John Henry Cardinal Newman, *An Essay on the Development of Christian Doctrine.* 6th ed. Notre Dame, IN: University of Notre Dame Press, 2011. E-book.

For surely I know the plans I have for you, says the Lord,
plans for your welfare and not for harm,
to give you a future with hope.
Then when you call upon me and come and pray to me,
I will hear you.
When you search for me, you will find me;
if you seek me with all your heart,
I will let you find me, says the Lord,
and I will restore your fortunes and gather you from all the nations
and all the places where I have driven you, says the Lord,
and I will bring you back to the place from which I sent you into exile.
(Jeremiah 29:11–14, NRSVA)

Thought for Reflection:

What is something in your life right now that requires you to have great faith to believe in a good outcome?

Five

Accepting Change

NO MATTER WHO we are, how we were raised, where we live, or what we do, life is a continual movement, a constant change. We move from total dependency as an infant in gradual steps toward adulthood and maturity as we age.

We eventually go to school and learn new things every day, and as we get older and a bit more mature our learning comes from what is going on around us, what we see, what we hear, and what we experience. Not everything we learn in our life journey is necessarily good for us, but even in the junk that we take in—the bad and the evil that we witness—we have the capacity to absorb great lessons that can make us better human beings, that can make our surroundings and those within them a little bit better off.

In so many ways, what we learn and how we deal with stuff is our choice. Change is one of the hardest things we have to learn to do throughout life, and it never seems to be an easy task. Yet, accepting change is our personal choice; no one can force us to change, nor can anyone make a change for us. We find some changes easier than others. Some can be made out of necessity or reasoned out.

A move from a single-bedroom apartment to a two-bedroom or a home may be the responsible thing to do when children arrive, or as they grow. One's career may require a move to a different city.

People who flee from their homelands, or even from their family members, most often do so out of fear for their safety or the safety of their loved ones.

Sometimes family situations dictate a very real need to put space and distance between members. No one should stay in any relationship where there is abusive behaviour in any way, shape, or form. Very often real healing within can only come after one removes oneself from the source.

We sometimes make other changes out of pure boredom with what we have, how we perceive ourselves or how we think others might perceive us. We like to have the latest gadgets—the smartest TVs, cell phones, or other electronic devices. We feel "better off" driving a new vehicle, or simply being able to go wherever we want and do whatever we want.

We make changes to our lifestyle habits, perhaps reluctantly, when we face health issues. We may have to struggle with dietary changes if we learn we have diabetes. We fight when told to hand in our driver's license when our eyesight deteriorates. We miss visiting family and friends when we are confined to our homes, for whatever reason.

But there are other changes that we need to make that are even more important. We must look at our habits and our behaviour on an ongoing basis. We try to be the best we can be for those around us, especially for those with whom we are in a relationship. So, too, we want to experience and enjoy the best relationship with God.

It is inherent within us to seek out and recognize God's presence in our lives and all of creation, and to allow it all to draw us into an ever-deepening relationship with God.

Since we are human, by our very nature we tend to look after ourselves—to think about "me" and "my" well-being. Because we are social beings, we strive to get along with others and to make friends. As part of entering into and sustaining those relationships, we try to follow the golden rule: not to do to anyone what we wouldn't like to be done to us.

As Christians, we believe that God reveals Himself to us and speaks to us most directly through the words and actions of others. So, while we work on our human relationships, we cannot separate those relationships from our relationship with God. And just as getting along with others can at times be difficult and iffy, so it can be with God. We can get so irritated with others that we may begin to complain, to gossip. We can get so caught up in what they have done, or what we perceive they have done, that we no longer see or even think that God is within them. In doing so, I think that we may be undercutting God's saving work in them, and God's work in ourselves through them.

We can get so caught up in the chaos of life that it gets us down. We might think we will find relief through self-medicating on drink, drugs, or any other addiction or vice. We can inflate our egos by pretending to be who we are not—by lying to others and hiding from ourselves the struggles life has challenged us with.

We can get so weighed down with shame and guilt over things we have done, or thought, that we may begin to think we are lost causes, that God wants nothing to do with us. Nothing could be further from the truth. God is our Creator. God formed and fashioned us, and He wants us to be whole—fully alive and accepting of who we are, even in our brokenness.

God is the source of all healing, and the power that can change our brokenness, our sinful ways, and our habits. No matter how hard we try on our own, we will fail unless we rely on God, the promises made by our Lord and Saviour Jesus Christ, and the power and grace of the Holy Spirit. God alone gives us the grace to accept the changes He wants to help us achieve, and the courage to enter into a *New Day*.

> We can get so weighed down with shame and guilt over things we have done, or thought, that we may begin to think we are lost causes, that God wants nothing to do with us. Nothing could be further from the truth.

Rather than wondering about or questioning
the direction your life has taken,
accept the fact that there is a path before you now.
Shake off the "whys" and "what ifs,"
and rid yourself of confusion.
Whatever was–is in the past.
Whatever is–is what's important.
The past is a brief reflection.

The future is yet to be realized.

Today is here.[7]

Thought for Reflection:

What are the dangers of regret and guilt?

Is there good that can come from this?

This is the word that came to Jeremiah from the Lord: "Go down to the potter's house, and there I will give you my message." So I went down to the potter's house, and I saw him working at the wheel. But the pot he was shaping from the clay was marred in his hands; so the potter formed it into another pot, shaping it as seemed best to him.

Then the word of the Lord came to me. He said, "Can I not do with you, Israel, as this potter does?" declares the Lord. "Like clay in the hand of the potter, so are you in my hand, Israel." (Jeremiah 18:1–6, NIV)

Thought for Reflection:

What would you like God to shape you into?

What colour and design would you like to have on you?

Whenever you feel flattened by life, do you blame yourself or do you think of God lovingly at work in you (painful though it may be)?

---

[7] Quotation by Vicki Silvers. Quoted by: Sue Atkins, "Why Embracing Change Is the Key to a Happier Life," https://sueatkinsparentingcoach.com/2021/08/today-my-son-becomes-a-man/

Six

Fear: Life's Alarm

Worry does not empty tomorrow of its sorrow. It empties today of its strength.[8]

THIS IS A very powerful statement, and we can easily substitute "worry" with "fear" without losing any of its meaning or power.

Wikipedia says that fear is the body's way of protecting itself from doing things that might be dangerous.[9]

Some writers use an acronym to define fear: **F**alse **E**vidence **A**ppearing **R**eal.[10]

Fears, no matter how they are defined, are real feelings at the moment of experience, and they can be intense. Throughout life, everyone has a particular fear—or perhaps more than one—that he or she has to face, deal with, or learn to live with. And there are many fears: fear of heights, fear of flying, fear of storms, fear of being alone, fear of confined or crowded spaces, fear of water, and fear of snakes or other animals, to name but a few.

These are specific and physical fears, but there are other types. Fear of failure, of being judged, of rejection, of bullying, of discrimination, or fear of losing everything (people or things) are some of the more emotional types of fears.

---

[8] Corrie Ten Boom. Quoted at goodreads.com/quotes/35574-worry-does-not-empty-tomorrow-of-its-sorrow-it-empties

[9] https://en.wikipedia.org/wiki/Fear

[10] Jon Gordon. "F.E.A.R. (False Evidence Appearing Real)," *Doulos Theo* (blog). Nov. 14, 2020. https://people.smu.edu/cgould/2020/11/14/f-e-a-r-false-evidence-appearing-real

Some fears relate more to society and justice, like the fear of facing racial, cultural, or religious prejudices, and fears related to inequalities and injustices seen on a local or global level.

Then there are the fears of doing or saying the wrong thing and hurting someone, or the fear of losing one's temper. To me, fears of this nature seem to fall into a different category: they are more a fear that others will feel pain or discomfort because of me.

Fear is a powerful inner emotion. While it can be an enemy that creates unimaginable havoc as it grows within and eventually paralyzes us, leaving us void of happiness and joy, it can also be a friend that can awaken, prepare, and strengthen us.

> To use fear as the friend it is, we must retrain and reprogram ourselves. We must persistently and convincingly tell ourselves that the fear is here—with its gift of energy and heightened awareness—so we can do our best and learn the most in the new situation.[11]

There is yet another, even more significant fear that society in general—and unfortunately many Christians, practicing Catholics included—fails to recognize or understand, and it is that fear that I want to focus on here: Fear of the Lord.

"Fear of the Lord" is one of the seven gifts of the Holy Spirit, along with wisdom, understanding, counsel, fortitude, knowledge, and piety.

How are we to understand fearing God as being a gift of the Holy Spirit—something offered freely to us from God?

This gift is sometimes misunderstood because of the word "fear." Our common understanding would imply that we ought to be afraid of God. Regrettably, many of my generation were brought up with a rather strict understanding of who God is: that He is a God who knows every single thing we do, and judges us accordingly. Now there is absolutely nothing wrong with any of that, but there is both a healthy fear of God and an unhealthy fear.

If we think of God only as a judge, knowing that we are sinners, then it follows that we can expect punishment from God for those things that we do that are not pleasing to Him—that break His commandments, that are in

---

[11] Peter McWilliams. Quoted at http://www.quotationspage.com/quote/29670.html

opposition to His plan for us. This is an unhealthy fear, and if that becomes our understanding of who God is, and how we picture Him in our lives, our focus goes more toward avoiding things we know to be wrong because we believe God will punish us, rather than toward doing right things, for which God desires to reward us with grace and with true satisfaction. Punishment from God just doesn't jive with a "gift," or anything else having to do with God.

Yes, God is a judge, but if we have a healthy fear of Him, then we know He is a just judge who knows our weaknesses and our inclinations to sin. He knows that we will try to do what pleases us at the moment, that we will snap back in self-defence of our own words and actions even when others correctly bring a wrongdoing to our attention. He knows our habits, and what we fall back on when we fail to see Him in our day—when we fail to identify our very life with that of Jesus.

Even in all of our missteps and our falls from grace, God remains always present, inviting us and waiting for us to turn to Him. His help and grace are always there. But we have to ask, and then accept what He offers. He will never push himself on us. He will never force us to accept what he desires to give us as a pure gift. Perhaps the condemnation God might have for us is if we consciously make a choice to publicly deny Him, turn away from Him, refuse to accept Him into our hearts and lives, and lead others to do the same.

So, what then is this "gift" of the "Fear of the Lord"?

The fear of the Lord is one of the most valuable possible gifts, a true and tangible treasure that we can receive. One aspect of this gift is that it establishes a relationship between God and His people, between God and you, and between God and me.

Those four words, fear of the Lord, all by themselves suggest a deep truth that acknowledges who we are in God's presence: that He alone is our God, and we are His people. God is our creator, and we are born in His very image and likeness. He knows what we need in life and what is best for our lives.

If we hope to live a life with true happiness, meaning, purpose, and mission, we have to ask that He strengthen our longing to walk side-by-side with Jesus and live our lives in a way that reflects His desire and plan for us. The stronger our relationship is with the Lord, the holier our fear of the Lord becomes. It is no longer something that primarily reflects a cautiousness, an expectation of retribution, but it becomes more that gift through which we can better recognize God's presence, and through it see that we are privileged to be so valued, loved, and cared for by God. It is that gift of an intimate relationship with God that we want to strive for.

The fear of the Lord entails giving up our control of life. It means surrendering, giving ourselves over to Him, and allowing God's very Spirit to fill our hearts and stir our spirits to joyfully choose His ways—to value, above all else, what He values. When we grow closer to valuing what God Himself values, this fear of the Lord takes on new meaning.

Accepting and acknowledging that we are children of a God who gives absolutely everything for our good changes our relationship. Knowing and believing that each of us is a daughter or son of God changes our perception of how God treats each one of us, and how we are to treat one another. Sure, we may still fear the punishment of hell should we die in a state of sin and separation from God. But isn't it our choice whether or not we allow sin to get in the way of that relationship?

Our fear of the Lord is not to be a dread of punishment or God's power. It is not needing to do something for God as though we were His slave. No, we are not slaves but sons and daughters, and as such our fear of the Lord is a deep desire in the very core of our heart to never offend God, because we know that He is all good and deserving of our love.

So how do I offend God? How do I sin?

Each one of the commandments given to Moses (and all humanity) directly from God is pretty straightforward. Jesus holds no punches in telling us what offends Him, the Father, and the Holy Spirit.

Jesus Himself, as recorded in St. Matthew's Gospel, spells out in no uncertain terms that when we harm, slander, or ignore others, or turn away from helping them in their needs, we offend and separate ourselves from God.

> *"For I was hungry and you gave me nothing to eat, I was thirsty and you gave me nothing to drink, I was a stranger and you did not invite me in, I needed clothes and you did not clothe me, I was sick and in prison and you did not look after me."*

They also will answer, "Lord, when did we see you hungry or thirsty or a stranger or needing clothes or sick or in prison, and did not help you?"

He will reply, "Truly I tell you, whatever you did not do for one of the least of these, you did not do for me." Then they will go away to eternal punishment, but the righteous to eternal life. (Matthew 25:42–46)

Our love for and relationship with God is a reflection of our love for and relationships with those we encounter every day.

Joanne and I were blessed to be in Rome in 2014 for our anniversary. One of the great blessings of that trip was being at our Holy Father's general audience on Wednesday, June 11. Pope Francis reflected on the fear of the Lord, and I quote the following three statements:

> Our love for and relationship with God is a reflection of our love for and relationships with those we encounter every day.

[Fear of the Lord] does not mean being afraid of God: we know well that God is Father, that He loves us and wants our salvation, and He always forgives, always; thus, there is no reason to be scared of him! Fear of the Lord, instead, is the gift of the Holy Spirit through whom we are reminded of how small we are before God and of His love and that our good lies in humble, respectful and trusting self-abandonment into His hands. This is fear of the Lord: abandonment in the goodness of our Father who loves us so much.[12]

Fear of the Lord is an "alarm." When man distances himself from God, when he takes advantage of everyone, when he lives attached to money, to vanity, to power or pride, the holy fear of God draws his attention: you will not be happy like this.[13]

---

[12] Pope Francis, General Audience, June 11, 2014
[13] Ibid.

This is the fear of God: abandonment into the goodness of Our Father who loves us so… This is what the Holy Spirit does in our hearts: He makes us feel like children in the arms of our Daddy… with the wonder and joy of a child who sees himself served and loved by his Father.[14]

Every believer and follower of Christ knows that there is a cost to being His disciple. Some may see this cost as having to give up certain freedoms or losing something of who we are. Pope Benedict XVI put it this way:

Are we not perhaps all afraid in some way? If we let Christ enter fully into our lives; if we open up ourselves totally to Him, are we not afraid that he might take something away from us? Afraid to give up something significant, or unique, that makes life beautiful? Do we risk ending up diminished, deprived of our freedom?

No, we lose nothing of what makes us free, beautiful and great. Only in this friendship are the doors of life opened wide, the potential of human existence revealed, do we experience beauty and liberation.[15]

Fear of the Lord is thus life's alarm that helps us further discover the awe, the wonder, and the goodness of the Lord, and better experience the fullness of whom we are created to be, with all beauty, joy, strength, and true freedom that God alone can give us.

But we have to be prayerfully careful to never use or take God's love and mercy for granted, for our own selfish means. Let's read that again: to never use or take God's love and mercy for granted, for our own selfish means. What do I mean by that?

Well, as we grow in faith, we begin to rely more and more on Christ our Lord, recognizing how He loves us and gave His life for our redemption and the forgiveness of our sins. We need to always distinguish between our reliance on God's goodness and taking His forgiveness for granted.

---

[14] "What Is the Fear of the Lord?," *Catholic Straight Answers*, https://catholicstraightanswers.com/fear-lord/

[15] Benedict XVI, "Mass, Imposition of the Pallium and Conferral of the Fisherman's Ring for the Beginning of the Petrine Ministry of the Bishop of Rome," delivered at St. Peter's Square, April 24, 2005.

We know without a doubt that God is always with us: He gave us his word. But in all truth, God cannot always depend on us—well, at least He can't depend on me always being with Him.

I am a sinner in need of God's love and compassion, and I rely on God's mercy. But I must be sincere in my contrition. I need to turn to our Saviour and Lord in humility and ask His pardon and His grace to strengthen me, so that I may listen to His whisper and avoid those things that tempt me to go where I should not go. I cannot simply ask for forgiveness, take it for granted that I have been forgiven, and then go back and repeat the same stuff. It is easy to fall, and when my time here on earth comes to an end, I want it to be when I fall on my knees in love and adoration, not when I have fallen under the weight of sin.

That recognition of my human weakness and God's unfathomable love is an example of what *fear of the Lord* is.

This gift, the healthy fear of the Lord, enables us to reflect our reverence and love of God by doing our utmost to follow closely all that Jesus taught us, to pray for the grace to avoid sin, and to fix our eyes on the things of heaven and not on material things here on earth, things that the world presents as must-haves.

This gift helps us develop and reflect a profound respect for the majesty of God. It helps us see ourselves as His creation, His "creatures." It enables us to depend upon Him, to have a true spirit of poverty, and never want to be separated from Him—He who is love.

This gift arouses in our souls a living sense of adoration and reverence for God, a sense of sorrow for our sins, and a real kind of expectation that God can and will reveal to us a *Newness every Day.*

Thought for Reflection:

My five top fears are:

1)

2)

Deacon Bob Hartman

3)

4)

5)

What is my single greatest fear in life?

Do I fear the Lord? What does that mean to me today?

There is no fear in love. But perfect love drives out fear, because fear has to do with punishment. The one who fears is not made perfect in love. (1 John 4:18, NIV)

Thought for Reflection:

How and when do I bring my fears to God?

How can love be the force to reduce and get rid of fear?

Seven

Struggle Is the Essence of Life

AS I'VE SAID before, life has its peaks and valleys. We can go from having wonderful experiences to times when life can be very chaotic. And very often we struggle—not so much with the chaos, but with how things can change so quickly, and in ways that we do not always understand or want to accept. Life is a marvellous gift, but it's a gift that often seems to come wrapped in varied forms of struggle.

There are times when our struggles get us down and wear us out. There are times when our struggles make us realize that life has taken on a "new norm," and for a while, that may infuriate us and make us miserable with ourselves and with others. These are the times that can draw us to God. These are those special occasions that can humble us, that can bring us to a point of desperation when we cry out, *"God, help me!"*

These are opportunities to let God be God and to allow ourselves to be children—His children. These are opportunities to allow God to be the loving Father that He so wants us to accept—the loving Father who will take control and resolve whatever is going on in a way that He knows to be best for us. God knows no other way of doing things.

A couple of years ago we brought some of our grandchildren to the remake of the film *The Lion King*. It's a wonderful Disney creation with many moral lessons to be learned. Although set in the animal kingdom, the film reflects the same type of struggles that humanity faces.

Many of our struggles flow from greed, rivalry, jealousy, and an all-pervasive attitude of entitlement to whatever we think we want or need to be happy. Many of life's struggles are brilliantly conveyed in the film as being part of the "Circle of Life" (its theme song).

Since our negative traits and habits are seldom life-giving, I would not go so far as to say they are part of the circle of life, but unfortunately, they are far too often the reality of what we encounter in life.

Right from birth, most people's lives center around resolutions of some sort or another. For example, the resolution to go from lying to sitting, from sitting to crawling, from crawling to walking, and eventually from walking to running.

That's usually the only way we make progress: some type of catalyzing force is needed to get us motivated, focused, and set on course.

The following brief article in the local newspaper a few years back addressed this very clearly:

I am twenty-six years old and my life is in part due to not just New Year's resolutions, but new day resolutions—resolutions to stay a course, to bring about a change, and to consistently struggle with myself.

As an Ahmadi Muslim, my faith teaches me that this is part of the essence of life—to struggle.[16]

Thought for Reflection:

Have you had to make certain resolutions that have helped you cope with struggles in life?

Were they one-shot resolutions or more like new everyday resolutions?

---

[16] Muneer Ahmad Khan, "Letter to the Editor," *London Free Press* (Jan. 5, 2013)

Come to me, all of you who are tired from carrying heavy loads, and I will give you rest. Take my yoke and put it on you, and learn from me, because I am gentle and humble in spirit; and you will find rest. For the yoke I will give you is easy, and the load I will put on you is light. (Matthew 11:28–30, GNT)

Thought for Reflection:

Some days, coping with life and illness might seem near impossible.

When I am experiencing darkness, do I find myself turning to God, or do I find it difficult to talk or pray to God?

What does God ask of me?

Is that an easy/light task, or somewhat overwhelming?

Looking for Help and Guidance

Eight
Help from Our Lady

AS I MENTIONED earlier, in June 2014, Joanne and I went to Rome. The preceding year had been quite stressful, with two family deaths, as well as the death of a dear friend and classmate, Deacon Doug. So at that particular time, we simply needed to get away, to spend some quality time on our own and with our Lord. It would also fulfill one of the items on our bucket list.

We arranged our trip so that we would be in Rome on Pentecost Sunday. This was also the first time that our wedding anniversary fell on Pentecost Sunday. So, when that day came, there we were in St Peter's Basilica, seated maybe a dozen rows from the front, close enough to get a full-length picture and video of Pope Francis as he incensed the altar at the beginning of Mass. And to add to the blessings of the day, we had met up with Fr. Peter Keller, who was studying there at the time, and he invited us to his home for lunch. We were met by several other priests who were also there for studies, and together they jointly offered us their blessings on our special day.

We spent a week in Rome, taking in many special sites beyond the Vatican and Sistine Chapel, and we certainly indulged in wonderful delicious Italian cuisine.

We shopped, of course, in some of the many small boutiques along the narrow side streets, with no shortage of religious goods on offer around the Vatican. In one of these stores, we discovered a beautiful prayer that we had never seen or heard of before.

It was a prayer to Our Lady Undoer of Knots, and it immediately touched both of us. We started saying it that very day and have made it part of our daily prayer life ever since. It is a prayer that asks our Blessed Mother to untwist, untie, and undo all those things in our lives that can rob us of our joy and zest, and in the void leave confusion, aches, pain, loneliness, emptiness, and many other emotions that leave a knot in the pit of the stomach.

These things can take a toll on our relationships with others, and also our relationship with God. They wear us down in discouragement and doubt, and leave us more susceptible to the workings of the evil one.

This prayer helps us to bring it all to our Lady, to entrust all of our knots to her motherly care with the certain belief that she will hold and ponder them in her heart, and bring them to her son on our behalf. We have Jesus' word on that: when on the cross, He looked at his mother and at the disciple He loved. He said to her, *"Behold your son,"* and to His disciple, *"Behold your mother"* (John 19:26–27). From the moment of Mary's "fiat," her declaration *"Let it happen to me as you have said"* (Luke 1:38, NLV), she agreed to being the point of entry of Christ our Saviour coming into our world and our lives. Her life was for Jesus. She followed Him in His public ministry, stood by Him and witnessed Him in His passion. She "pondered it all in her heart." In this passage Jesus firms up our relationship with Mary—that she is to us as she is to Him, that she is with us as she is with Him. To me, Jesus not only set Mary to be our Mother, but a helper, an intercessor—someone who prays and brings our petitions to God.

Some of the knots that we hold in our hearts are twisted so tightly that it can be painful as Mother Mary tugs at them. Yet in her gentle maternal care, little by little she helps us; with those things we find hard to let go of, she helps us carry and cope until we can give them up.

I invite you to take this prayer into your daily life. It is reproduced below. I would also encourage you to check the web for the Novena to Our Lady Undoer of Knots. As more and more of our knots get unravelled, we become more and more able to truly enter into every *New Day* we are gifted with.

O Immaculate Lady
Undoer of Knots,
Pray for us!

O Virgin Mary, faithful Mother
who never refuses to come to the aid of your children;
Mother whose hands never cease to help,
because they are moved by the loving kindness
that exists in your Immaculate Heart,
cast your eyes of compassion upon me,
and see the snarl of knots that exists in my life.
You know all the pains and sorrows
caused by these tangled knots.
Mary, my Mother,
I entrust to your loving hands the entire ribbon of my life.
In your hands there is no knot which cannot be undone.

Most holy Mother, pray for Divine assistance to come to my aid.
Take this knot (mention need) into your maternal hands this day;
I beg you to undo it for the glory of God,
once and for all, in the name of your Divine Son,
Jesus Christ. Amen.[17]

Thought for Reflection:

What is there in my life:

That has my gut tied up in knots?

That keeps me from feeling fully alive?

That gets in the way of my relationship with others? With God?

---

[17] www.CatholicPrayerCards.org, Card #316

Nine

Ephphatha—Be Opened!

ONE OF MY favourite spiritual writers is John Ortberg, an American Presbyterian minister.

In his book *Soul Keeping,*[18] he tells the story of how farmers in the Midwest used to tie a rope from their houses to their barns at the first sight of a blizzard. They knew stories of people who had died in their own yards during a white-out because they couldn't find their way home.

There are many blizzards in life that can cause fear and frenzy, raise many questions, make us suspicious and doubtful, and may even cause us to shy away—even from those we have always placed great trust and hope in. We can get lost in the storms of life. What we need is a rope from the back door to the barn as we find our way home again.

It's difficult to live out our faith journey in today's world. Everything we see and hear paints success as having it all—youth, health, everything at our fingertips, being in need of nothing.

But we also see and hear all the bad stuff: the hatred and prejudice, the evil in the world, society, and even in our Church.

If we want to continue to grow in our journey of faith, we need encouragement—and lots of it. We should look for encouragement from family and friends.

---

[18] Grand Rapids, MI: Zondervan, 2014.

But if we are to grow in faith, then we need to listen to the voice of God, not only from those we trust, but most of all through Sacred Scripture.

In Isaiah 35:4–7, Isaiah faces the people of Israel who are discouraged as they taste the bitterness of exile in Babylon. He says to them: Be strong, do not fear. Here is your Lord. He will come and save you, and then the blind will see and the deaf will hear.

Mark 7:31–37 speaks to us of Jesus's journey into Gentile territory near the Sea of Galilee. A man who is deaf and with some kind of speech impediment is brought to him. Jesus takes the man aside, puts His fingers into his ears, spits, and touches his tongue. Then looking up to heaven, He says, *"Ephphatha—be opened,"* and immediately the man can hear and speak plainly.

And James 2:1–5 warns us not to make distinctions between people. God's love, mercy, and favour are not only for the Jewish people but for all humanity.

God opens our ears so that we may hear His voice. He frees our tongues so that we may proclaim His Word. And He heals our paralysis—all those things that shut us down and close off our hearts—so that we may walk in His ways.

In Jesus, the words of Isaiah are fulfilled and come to life: *"For waters shall break forth in the wilderness, and streams in the desert"* (Isaiah 35:6, NRSVA).

Today, you and I, and the whole of our Catholic Church, face a great blizzard. The evil of sexual abuse and how it was covered up creates a terrible storm and division. In the past, many of us may have wanted to deny the thought of such things happening. Today we cannot—we simply know better.

This is a real crisis in the Church. It undermines and calls into question the integrity of all the great works done through the Church by people of faith.

We all feel great shame and anger that these evil and criminal deeds were committed by some who made solemn vows to treat and serve God's people as Christ always did: in faith, truth, love, and compassion. We all hurt. It affects all of us who profess and try to live out our faith in Jesus Christ as baptized Catholic Christians.

We pray that the Truth comes to light. Only when we allow light to illumine the darkness can we begin to accept God's grace to move forward.

Our hearts and our prayers go out to everyone who has ever suffered the violence of sexual, physical, or emotional abuse. These sins by clergy trigger memories and take victims back to relive a traumatic point in their lives.

We need to focus and pray for our children and grandchildren, who are greatly impacted by what they see and hear. How are we responding to them?

Scripture doesn't explain why Jesus took the deaf man in the Gospel aside. But Jesus was always sensitive to the needs of all who came to him. It's easy to imagine that this man felt threatened by people. He couldn't hear them, but he saw their expressions. He could see that they were making fun of him and laughing at him. He must have wondered what they were saying about him. Jesus honoured his dignity and listened to him privately.

That's our challenge today. To listen, accept, and respect what others, including our children, have to say; to free them to speak their thoughts, their concerns, their doubts; and to respond.

God's Word calls us to be open so that we may see and hear what's going on around us; so we can see each other's pain, each other's need to be heard and accepted, with Christ-like love and deep respect.

In God, our tongues can be freed to speak words of welcome, words of comfort, and words of healing, if we open our hearts and allow the waters of truth and compassion to flow in the desert.

Jesus is the rope we need to affix to our hearts, to cling to firmly, and to draw us to eternal life.

Christ our Saviour is here, and He has a message for every one of us.

Be open to meeting challenges as opportunities.

Be open to new experiences in our relationship with God.

Be open to the dawn of a *New Day*.

Ephphatha—Be Opened!

Thought for Reflection:

How is God asking me to be open to Him today?

No one has ever seen, no one has ever heard, no one has ever imagined what God has prepared for those who love him. (1 Corinthians 2:9, ERV)

I pray that the eyes of your heart may be enlightened in order that you may know the hope to which he has called you, the riches of his glorious inheritance in his holy people... (Ephesians 1:18, NIV)

If you abide in me, and my words abide in you, ask whatever you wish, and it will be done for you. (John 15:7, ESV)

Thought for Reflection:

What do I imagine God has in store for me?

Do I have hope that I will ever truly know and receive what God has in mind for me?

How am I living my life in a way that reflects God's Word?

Ten

Prayer, Gratitude, and Forgiveness

WHEN I WROTE this, it was just after Thanksgiving weekend here in Canada.

Every day gives us plenty to be grateful for. We humans get accustomed to things, and we take far too much for granted. Every day ought to have at least several moments when we just sit back and appreciate all that we have, showing gratitude for everything God has given to us. In fact, it would be better if every day was full of such gratitude.

All we are—all we have—is a gift from God our Father, beginning with life itself. God formed us long before we came into being. God breathed life into us upon our birth. To every single person who has ever lived, regardless of gender, colour, race, size, shape, or any other characterization we so often use to label people and put them into boxes, God has given the gift of dignity. Each one of us is a child of God, so loved by God that He sent His only Son to be one of us in all things but sin.

God gave us life, and through His Son has set us free. Through the life of Jesus Christ, through His total commitment and surrender to God, His Father, we have been so blessed and so privileged to be able to know firsthand the Father's unconditional, boundless love for every one of us. Through Jesus's own words and actions, as given to us in Sacred Scripture, we are invited to follow Christ, to hear His words and observe His actions, to see and know for ourselves God's love, mercy, and care for every single individual. God gives us the grace, strength, and courage to follow Christ, to live lives that reflect His. If we accept all that God desires to give us, then we too have the capacity and ability to offer ourselves in full surrender and service to God—and we will want to.

Many of us like to think that we can do things on our own. After all, we have the knowledge, vision, and ability to process our thoughts in whatever circumstance we find ourselves in. And if we can't figure it out on our own, we can tap into the know-how of professionals simply by searching the internet or turning to YouTube for clear step-by-step tutorials.

"Vanity of vanities," Scripture says of our independence, our self-reliance, our pride (Ecclesiastes 1:2, NRSVA).

We are social beings. The book of Genesis tells us that after God created man, He formed woman, equal in status, to be his companion, and he hers. We need one another if we are ever to become whole and fully live the life God has given us to live.

This means we have to come to accept one another—to recognize and appreciate God's presence in every person, no matter how different they may be. God is there: even for that person who has treated us unfairly, who has judged us without knowing us, and whom we find offensive and repelling. God is present to that person in the very same way He is present to you and me. To recognize and feel God's presence, we have to allow Him in, still and quiet ourselves, and pray.

Praying is talking to God as a friend. In prayer, we thank God for who He is, for being our creator, and for sending Jesus to be our saviour and redeemer. And in prayer, we share what's been going on in life, the good, the typical chaos of the day, and any particular sin, habit, situation, person, or group that we are struggling with. Sometimes it may seem like we are complaining to God, and that may well be the case—and that's okay.

Jesus, in His humanity, knows all about chaos, opposition, and rejection, and about any struggle we may be experiencing.

God loves us right where we are, and if that's being in a sour mood, so be it. But He loves us too much to leave us there. He wants us to know that we are never alone and that He will never abandon us. God wants to shower us with His love, with His compassion, and with His mercy. He wants us to be rid of all the things that interfere with our relationship with Him, spending time with Him, sharing our life with Him, and loving Him.

Just before dying, Jesus cried out from the cross, *"I thirst"* (John 19:28, ESV). He was telling the world that He thirsts for humanity to turn to Him, to love Him, and perhaps more than anything to accept the tremendous gift of what He came to do: the gift of what He was enduring on the cross for us, the gift of freely laying down His life that we may have full access to God our Father and inherit a place in God's kingdom. I think one of the greatest sins we can commit is to deny the love God has for us.

Unfortunately, Catholic guilt is real, and it's easy to get entrapped in. Most of the time, we know when we do wrong—when we say or do things that go against what we know in faith to be what God wants of us. That's what sin is.

We know our sins, and we tell God we are sorry, yet we go back to them again and again. St. Paul wrote in his letter to the Church of Rome, *"I do not understand what I do. For what I want to do I do not do, but what I hate I do"* (Romans 7:15, NIV).

Like St. Paul, we don't understand our behaviour either.

We can get so discouraged and down on ourselves that we begin to think that God must be getting fed up with us. Surely He won't forgive us again. Why would He?

To me, that is placing human limitations on God. That is denying God's unconditional love and desire to forgive. That is about as close as one can get to denying that Jesus suffered and died so that we might be freed from sin.

We read in the Gospel of St. John, *"For God so loved the world that he gave his one and only Son, that whoever believes in him shall not perish but have eternal life"* (John 3:16, NIV).

God doesn't expect us to be perfect from the get-go. All we need to do is believe in Jesus Christ; He alone will do the perfecting, not us.

Forgiving someone who has hurt us is often a very difficult thing to do. But very often it is equally difficult to be on the receiving end of forgiveness. We sometimes doubt. Can this person put it behind himself or herself?

Forgiveness from God can also be tricky. I firmly believe that if we ask God to forgive our sins and our wrongdoing, He *will*. Yes, we need to go to God with a proper attitude, a true resolve to do better and to put God first and rely on His help. But God forgives.

I have long tried to end my day with the Ignatian practice of a daily examen: a prayer reflecting on the events of the day, and what God has asked of me this day. Where or in whom did I recognize God's presence? More to the point, in what situation or in whom did I fail to see the presence of God? Part of my prayer before I close my eyes includes recalling my failings this day, my *mea culpas,* followed by saying the Jesus prayer three times: "Lord Jesus Christ, Son of God, have mercy on me, a sinner." After doing this for some time I began to feel a stirring within, a sense that God was telling me something.

Reflecting on one's failings can leave a person feeling empty, and it was in the sheer quiet of that emptiness that God was saying to me: "It's good, Bob, that you realize your shortcomings, your impatience, your anger, your sinfulness, and it's even better that you bring all that to Me. Yes, you are a sinner, but you are far more than that. Don't let your weaknesses paralyze you. You are my child, my son whom I dearly love, and I have great things for you to do, great things in store for you, for you are to mirror My presence to others. Rest in My love."

This seems to be an ongoing message that God wants me to reflect on, trust in, and be strengthened in. And those nights when I am just too tired, or simply don't want to think about the events of the day, there is that little whisper in my ear: "Bob, are you forgetting something? It is good for you to spend a little time thinking about the day, and how I have been right there with you."

Our inability to let go of our feelings of guilt reflects our doubts and our questions. We may not believe in the depths of our hearts that God loves us so completely that He does indeed have endless mercy. After all, how—or better yet, why—would God forgive me over and over and over again?

This unfailing, never-ending *love* that the Father has for us is pure mystery: not something that we can comprehend, but rather something we are to believe, to simply accept. We need to acknowledge God's gift that we are His daughters, His sons.

> We need to acknowledge God's gift that we are His daughters, His sons. Then we can feel the peace of having been forgiven, start afresh, and truly give thanks and praise.

Then we can feel the peace of having been forgiven, start afresh, and truly give thanks and praise.

God desires to lift us up—to help us rise above our guilt, our fears, and our painful relationships—but because we have this doubt, we just keep trying to fix ourselves. We imagine that we can overcome our sins, our bad habits, and our brokenness on our own.

We know what happens when we do that. We keep spinning our wheels, feeling good because we beat it one day, only to give in once again the next. We cannot do it on our own—we need God's help. We need to turn to sincere prayer, and ask the Holy Spirit to give us the grace we need:

The grace and humility to recognize our inabilities and to accept God's freeing love

The grace to desire to listen, hear, and come to know what God is trying to say to us at any given time, what He is asking of us

The grace of humility and gratefulness to receive, accept, and rejoice in God's undying love

The grace to know who God is, and who we are

The grace to realize that God alone can turn this day into a New Day.

I make all things new. (Revelation 21:1–5, ASV)

Thought for Reflection:

What do Prayer, Gratitude, and Forgiveness have to do with this very brief line from Revelation?

Does gratitude simply open me to God's work within me, or does it present a real challenge and a deeper desire and wanting for the Almighty to do all that He wants to do within me?

Eleven

Beginning Each Day with a Song of Praise

SACRED SCRIPTURE TELLS us that after Zechariah named his son John, his mouth was opened and he began praising God. He and Elizabeth were old, and had long given up on being able to have a child. And when the angel announced that they would have a son, Zechariah, knowing they were both old, questioned the possibility, and in his doubt, he was made mute.

After the birth of their child, when pressed by family and friends as to the child's name, Zechariah wrote: *He is called John.* Immediately he was able to speak again. Filled with the Spirit of the Lord, Zechariah began to praise God and declare his belief in all that had been told of Him.

This canticle, often referred to as the Benedictus or Song of Blessing, is Zechariah's song of thanksgiving:

Blessed be the Lord, the God of Israel; he has come to his people to set them free.

He has raised up for us a mighty saviour, born of the house of David.

Through his holy prophets, he promised of old that he would save us from our enemies, from the hands of all who hate us.

He promised to show mercy to our fathers and to remember his holy covenant.

This was the oath he swore to our father Abraham: to set us free from the hands of our enemies, free to worship him without fear, holy and righteous in his sight all the days of our life.

You, my child, shall be called the prophet of the Most High, for you will go before the Lord to prepare his way, to give his people knowledge of salvation by the forgiveness of their sins.

In the tender compassion of our God, the dawn from on high shall break upon us, to shine on those who dwell in darkness and the shadow of death, and to guide our feet into the way of peace.[19]

This prayer is said every day by all who follow the Liturgy of the Hours, and it is very fitting that the Church has placed it in the morning Liturgy of this prayer of the Church. It is a prayer that helps us enter into each new day with an awareness of who God is, of His covenant with us, what He wants to give us, how we are to respond, and what we are to do with His gifts during the remaining hours of our day.

Let's look closer at this canticle.

The first five verses bestow all blessings and glory on the Lord.

Blessed be the Lord, the God of Israel, the God of our homeland. He has come to do what He had promised in scripture: to set us free from sin and the darkness of death. Born out of the house (lineage) of David, He has been raised up to be for us a great saviour. God gave words to the prophets right from the beginning, telling us that He will save us from harm, that He will remember everything He promised: that He will be our God, and we His people, and He will show mercy to all our ancestors who have died. God made a solemn oath to Abraham that He would indeed free us—not only from those who oppose us, but even more importantly, that we would be free to worship God without fear, and that we would be holy and righteous people forevermore.

In the last two verses of the canticle, Zechariah speaks words of prophecy to his newborn son John (the Baptizer): "My child, you will become known as God's prophet. You are to go ahead of the Lord. You are to prepare the way

---

[19] Luke 1:68–79, as quoted in *Christian Prayer: The Liturgy of the Hours*, New York: Catholic Book Publishing Co., 1976.

for him. You are to tell His people that the Lord is very near; tell them that they are to repent and straighten out their lives, and that the Lord is coming to bring them salvation through the forgiveness of all their sins and offences against God and against one another. Make it known that God's great love and compassion will shine upon them and on all who live in darkness and the fear of death, and He will teach and lead all who believe to live in a way of peace."

What a wonderful prayer with which we can enter into each *New Day*. It brings to our minds all that God has given us, how He constantly sustains us, and everything He has promised to us. For we are His people, the flock He has chosen as His own.

Oh, how we need to be reminded—perhaps even more so on those days when we encounter and face the varied and inevitable clouds of life. Hearing those reassuring words that God has an everlasting covenant with us—a covenant of love, compassion, and mercy—we are far better equipped to face whatever we might have to face on any given day.

We are strengthened in our resolve to be fully alive in our discipleship with Christ, to be cognizant of our responsibilities as baptized people of faith, to lay out for others the way to the Lord, and to help our brothers and sisters know of God's love, God's healing grace, God's forgiveness of all sins.

So very often we see our world as being so very messed up. In our baptism, we became sons and daughters of God, heirs to the Kingdom. Our role as Christians is to bring Christ's light, compassion, and love to everyone we encounter each day.

We pray for the grace to bring others to God by our example, and to do so in even the most difficult times. That is our greatest contribution to world peace, each and every *New Day* of our lives.

Thought for Reflection:

Pray Zechariah's canticle, the Benedictus, very slowly, quietly and reflectively. Allow it to sit and move within you, to speak to your heart.

How does my life reflect my belief that Christ has come to set me free, that He can save me from all that sin and darkness might deliver, that in His compassion and forgiveness, I might live a life that is holy and righteous and accept His invitation into the Kingdom of heaven?

How does my life reflect my call by God to be a prophet, to joyfully and unashamedly share the Good News that I have received with others, so that they also may recognize, accept, and love the Lord each day of their life?

Twelve

Our Magnificat

FOR A LONG time, one of my favourite prayers has been the one Mary prayed when she met with her cousin Elizabeth and shared with her the great peace and joy that God had filled her with.

> My soul proclaims the greatness of the Lord,
> and my spirit rejoices in God my Savior,
> for He has looked with favour on my lowliness.
> Henceforth all generations will call me blessed;
> for the mighty God has done great things for me, and holy is His name.
> And His mercy is on those who fear him from generation to generation.
> He has shown strength with his arm,
> He has scattered the proud in the imagination of their hearts,
> He has put down the mighty from their thrones,
> and has lifted up the lowly;
> He has filled the hungry with good things,
> and the rich He has sent empty away.
> He has helped His servant Israel, in remembrance of His mercy,
> as He spoke to our fathers,
> to Abraham and to His descendants forever.[20]

_____

[20] Luke 1:46–56 (from *Christian Prayer: The Liturgy of the Hours*)

Mary didn't just say this prayer to God without a purpose. She was awestruck and filled with gratitude and joy that God had looked upon her lowliness; that He would fulfill His promise to humankind through her son. Mary recognized she had been chosen to play a major role in God's plan of salvation for the whole world.

In the Magnificat, I believe Mary was also telling everyone that God has given each of us a role to play in His plan of salvation—that God's promise to us will come to full fruition if we listen to His Word and live our lives as He directs us to.

We are commissioned through baptism to proclaim the greatness of the Lord. Our spirits are meant to rejoice in God—the One who breathed into us the very breath of life, the One who gave us His Son Jesus for the forgiveness of our sins and our weaknesses, the One who offers us eternal life through the salvation of our souls.

This is our faith, and in our faith, we can claim Mary's prayer, this beautiful song of praise, as our own. It ought to be the song of every person who recognizes their own sinfulness and has experienced God's compassion, mercy, and forgiveness. God cleanses our consciences every time we go to Him with sincere hearts, sincere sorrow for our sins, and a true and deep resolve to do our absolute best to remain faithful and avoid those people and things that tempt us.

We can always bring our prayers, our concerns, our gratitude, and our needs—no matter how scrambled they may be—to Mother Mary, knowing that she will hold and ponder them in her heart and bring them to her son on our behalf.

Each time we experience God's forgiveness, our hearts and minds are opened to begin to see how deeply God loves us personally, despite our weaknesses, our failings, and our doubts.

God has indeed looked with favour on my lowliness. Despite all my failings and sins, God always offers me his mercy and love. Thus far, God has repeatedly given me new beginnings, *New Days*. I don't know how many days or years I may have left, but I know that if I call upon His help, trust and rely on His bountiful grace, and live my life accordingly, then in His time, He will invite me into his Kingdom where I too will be called blessed.

Thus, the Magnificat is the prayer Mary gives to all of us who desire to be followers and disciples of her Son. The more we are able to take this prayer to heart, the more we will be able to rejoice in life, in God our Saviour. Then we can look forward to every *New Day,* so we can live God's Word in our lives ever more fully, and be more open, more encouraging, and more present to those whom we encounter throughout our life journey.

Thought for Reflection:

Take time to read the Magnificat very slowly and deliberately. Reflect on each line.

What does it mean to you?

How does it relate to your life?

What does it say to you about God's love for you personally?

Example:

Just how do I proclaim God's greatness in my everyday life?
What are some of the great things God has done for me?
When has God lifted me and satisfied my hunger?

Our Ultimate Source

Thirteen

Do This in Memory of Me
Our Great Commission

OUR LORD JESUS, in complete surrender and obedience to His Father, gave us a blueprint, a road map. It leads not only toward our final destination, a place he has prepared for us in the Kingdom of Heaven, but shows the way to live our lives fully, with peace and happiness, in the here and now.

Christ made it perfectly clear that following God's will is not an easy road to follow. We will endure pain and suffering. But Jesus our Lord made promises to us: that we will never be left on our own, that He will be with us always, that the Holy Spirit will guide us and walk us through everything, good and bad, and that nothing—no one—given Him by the Father would ever be lost.

Jesus also gave us the great gift of celebrating who He was and is: celebrating His unconditional love for everyone, especially those on the fringes of society, the poor, the ignored and forgotten; His message to the world; the way He freely accepted and bore the burden of the sins of all humankind, for all ages; His passion, crucifixion, and resurrection from the dead.

We celebrate the mystery of His love for us every time we participate in the celebration of Holy Mass, where we are fed by God's Word, and by His very being at the table of the Eucharist. God reveals Himself more and more as we listen, hear, and take into our being every word that has been given to us through Christ, and then receive Jesus Himself, the Bread of Life, in Holy Communion.

Jesus calls us to Himself at every Eucharist, just as He called Zacchaeus: *"I must stay at your house today"* (Luke 19:5, ESV).

Jesus wants to live in our hearts. He wants us to welcome Him into our everyday activities, and wants us to accept and receive His love and all He desires to give us. Jesus wants us to truly believe and reflect on His words: *"... you are a chosen race, a royal priesthood, a holy nation, God's own people..."* (1 Peter 2:9, NRSVA).

We have the surety that it is possible, by the grace of God, to give up our pride and our self-reliance and surrender all we are to God, trusting in His promises.

That is our faith—our strength, hope, and anticipation for each new day. It is in that faith, that strength, hope, and anticipation, that we welcome with joy and excitement every new day we are given. There we find our purpose, our mission: to grow ever more intimate with our Lord and Saviour, our brother Jesus, and follow His lead toward eternal salvation: for ourselves, for those we love, and indeed the whole of humankind. For there we will experience in the light of God the true *New Day.*

> *Lord, I am not worthy*
> *that you should enter under my roof*
> *but only say the word*
> *and my soul shall be healed.*[21]

Thought for Reflection

We hear and pray these words at every celebration of the Eucharist, just before the reception of Holy Communion.

It is a prayer in which, first of all, we come before God in humility. We acknowledge our unworthiness to be in God's presence, let alone to have Him enter into our very being, the heart and soul of our existence. But in these words, we also

---

[21] Matthew 8:8, as quoted in *The Roman Missal,* Canadian edition. Ottawa, ON: Concacan, 2011.

declare our trust and faith in God's love, revealed to us through Jesus Christ, and made alive in us through the power of the Holy Spirit. We profess with childlike belief: Just say the word, and I will be okay, I will be healed.

What is my mindset when I approach the table of the Lord to receive Jesus in Holy Communion?

What is my mindset in the minutes after receiving Jesus?

What does receiving Jesus, in Word and in Eucharist, commission me to do in the minutes and days that follow?

Father,
Remember your holy covenant,
Sealed with the blood of the Lamb.
Forgive the sins of your people
And let this new day
bring us closer to salvation.[22]

Thought for Reflection

What exactly is God's covenant with you?

---

[22] *Christian Prayer: Liturgy of the Hours,* Wednesday, week IV.

Fourteen
Get Up and Eat!

I am the bread of life… But here is the bread that comes down from heaven, which anyone may eat and not die. (John 6:48, 50, NIV)

I LOVE TO eat, and breakfast is my favourite meal, so I welcome this invitation of Jesus to get up and eat. And the menu he lays out before me is appealing, exciting, and satisfying.

There are many references in Sacred Scripture, like the one above, of Jesus being the true source of nourishment for humankind.

In the Book of Kings, Elijah is worn out and pleads to the Lord to take his life. But God sends an angel to tell Elijah that the purpose of his life has not yet been filled: *"Get up and eat, or the trip will be too much for you"* (1 Kings 19:7, GNT).

I don't know about you, but I need all the nourishment I can get to give me strength in my life journey. While food and drink are essential to keep our bodies functioning, love, friendship, companionship, and our innate thirst to learn are among the essential ingredients to nourish our minds.

Of equal or greater importance for a full and rich life is to have our hearts and souls fed on a regular ongoing basis. Eucharist, Sacred Scripture, and other wholesome reading are the prime sources that feed my faith. They help give me a clearer, brighter, and more peaceful attitude. I share with you some of the passages that grace me with the extra strength I need to maneuver through the peaks and valleys of the roller-coaster journey of life. Perhaps they, or other passages, will provide some food for thought for you as well.

In St. Paul's letter to the Ephesians (4:30–5:2), he tells them that with God's grace and power, they can put away all their bad habits and attitudes; overcome bitterness and anger and become kind, giving, and forgiving; and that they can live in love. St. Paul says that is how we are to taste and see the Lord's goodness in our everyday lives.

For me, Psalm 34:8 (NIV) is a direct appeal to our senses of hunger, taste and sight: *"Taste and see that the Lord is good…"*

A few verses before the quote I began this part with, John 6:1–15 records the account of the multiplication of the loaves and fish. It reveals God as the great provider of all our needs.

A few verses later in John's Gospel, Jesus confronts the crowds that followed Him: *"…you are looking for me, not because you saw signs I performed but because you ate the loaves and had your fill"* (John 6:26, NIV).

He challenges them, and us, to open our hearts. While He does indeed want to fill our bellies with good food and drink, what He offers is so much more, and He spells it out: *"I am the bread of Life. Whoever comes to me will never go hungry, and whoever believes in me will never be thirsty"* (John 6:35, NIV).

Then in John 6:48–51 (NIV), Sacred Scripture continues with this very same message that Jesus is our everyday nourishment.

I am the bread of life. Your ancestors ate the manna in the wilderness, yet they died. But here is the bread that comes down from heaven, which anyone may eat and not die. I am the living bread that came down from heaven. Whoever eats this bread will live forever. This bread is my flesh, which I will give for the life of the world.

In John 6:54 (NIV), we hear Jesus elaborate further on His being the living bread that will give eternal life to all who believe: *"Whoever eats my flesh and drinks my blood has eternal life, and I will raise them up at the last day."*

Scripture repeatedly speaks to us of Jesus filling all of our needs, telling us that He is the Bread of Life, the living bread. This is an important and fundamental message that God wants us to hear and take to heart.

What does it mean to us?

What is God asking of you and me?

Are we that different from the crowds who followed Jesus because He filled their bellies?

How often are our prayers centred on asking God to help us, to give us what we think we need, what we think could make life easier for us and for those we care for?

If we want true and lasting happiness and joy in this life, we need our hearts, our spirits, and our souls nourished by the Words and Presence of Jesus Christ, our Lord and our God. This hunger is far more in need of being satisfied then our desire to have our bellies, our homes, or our garages filled.

"Get up and eat" is an invitation to partake in the life of Christ, but it is also a call to action: *Get up!*

In these authoritative words, there is an urgency: a push to get us moving, to take the steps we need to take to move away from complacency, to turn our backs on our egos and desires, and to be still and quiet long enough to encounter God face-to-face in His Word, in Eucharist, and yes, even in the loneliness, the frustration, and the varied and painful needs of others. To *get up* requires a conscious decision to move toward an ever-deepening relationship with God. Are we that different from those who knew Jesus only as the carpenter, the son of Mary? Do we accept and take in all His Words that He is the bread that came down from heaven?

I know I often fail to recognize Jesus in the struggles, the chaos, and the routine of daily life—especially when things don't go as I would like. Yet, again and again, Jesus reminds us that He came to feed us through His Words and through His deeds. He wants nothing more than to feed our bodies, our minds, our hearts and our souls with His very being.

Why? Because He loves us. Because *He wants us* to *love Him*—to trust Him, to rely on His grace, mercy, and forgiveness, and to one day enjoy eternal life in heaven where we will see Him face-to-face. That's why He endured all He did for us, why He died for us, and why He rose from the dead: to show us that this life we have been given has purpose and meaning. As tough, demanding and messy as life can often be, we have a God who calls us to Himself to rise in glory with Him and to spend eternity with Him. That's our destiny.

But our journey to eternity is not meant to be easy. We have our doubts, as did those who couldn't understand how Jesus could possibly be the bread of life. Being Christian does not give us any exemption from the physical, emotional, or spiritual pains and struggles of life.

There are times when we can get caught up in what happens to us. We may define ourselves in terms of what's going on in our lives, but we are far more than simply physical beings. We are infused with a soul, with the presence of God Himself. We are God's beloved, meant to live in communion with Him and with one another; we are invited to accept all that God wants to give us: the gift of life, our own and that of others, and the gift of the Holy Spirit, ever present to guide and direct our lives if we but ask. We *need* our faith in God, our faith in salvation and redemption, to feed us and to nourish us on our journey to be with God in the here and now, and for eternity.

Today and every day, we are reminded that God calls and invites us—you and me—to Himself. And we have new opportunities to respond in humility, to turn away from anything that separates us from Him, and to listen.

God surely will talk to us, but we have to want to hear:

Come to Me.
Don't be afraid.
Come and give Me everything that troubles you, that weighs you down.
Lay your failings and sins at My feet. Trust in My mercy.
I am with you and I want to fill you with peace.
I want to give you all that you need.
I want to give you Me.
Come, get up and eat!

Thought for Reflection:

Name your greatest need right now: what you hunger for the most from God.

Who or what gives me the push and encouragement I need to search for, receive, and accept all that our Lord wants to give me to feed all my needs?

Moving Forward

Fifteen

Evangelization

EVANGELIZATION IS SHARING the Good News proclaimed by Jesus in ways that touch the minds and hearts of others. Sharing our own experience of God can help others soften their attitudes, and change their hearts and minds to follow Him.

In the Gospel of Mark 10:2–6 (NCB), we find Jesus doing precisely that. We are told that while Jesus was teaching the crowds, there were some who tried to trap Him, questioning Him on matters of divorce. They said, *"Moses allowed a man to write a certificate of divorce and dismiss her."* But Jesus said to them, *"It was because of the hardness of your hearts that he wrote this commandment for you."*

To me, this leads to the next few verses of Mark (10:17–30), in which a rich young man approached Jesus and asked what he must do to inherit eternal life. By all accounts, he was a good person who seemed to have it all. He ran up to Christ and knelt before Him, appearing eager to hear God's word. He claimed to have kept the commandments all his life. Maybe he was proud of his behaviour, looking for a bit of praise. Maybe he simply wanted to add one more good thing to his resume: being a disciple of Jesus. Was he testing Jesus too?

Christ knew something was lacking, and told the man that he was missing *"one thing."* Jesus looked at him, loved him, and called him to do something different, something more, something he hadn't been doing: Sell all you have, give the money to the poor, then follow Me.

Jesus asked this man, who had done nothing bad, to do something good—to put into practice the greatest commandments of loving God and loving his neighbour as himself. It was not enough that he had done no wrong—he had to do right as well; he had to love and put love into practice.

You and I try to live good lives, to do nothing bad, and to keep the commandments. Yet Christ invites us to do more: to truly love, to generously give, and to follow Him. Everything He asked of the young man, He asks of us. We who hear the Word of God, the Good News, are called to share that message of salvation with others.

As Christians, that is our mission. That is what evangelization is all about. We come to Church, to Mass, to be renewed in spirit and transformed bit-by-bit by the Word of God and the Eucharist into true and faithful disciples of Jesus. And at the end of every Mass, we hear the words, "Go in peace, glorifying the Lord by your life," or, "Go and announce the gospel by how you live."

The man in Mark's Gospel turned and walked away from Christ's invitation to follow Him. His possessions had become his pride, accomplishment, security, and idol. He failed to take seriously the very first commandment.

Jesus, saddened as the man left, said, *"How hard it is for the rich to enter the kingdom of God!"* (Mark 10:23, NIV).

So what things, what personal possessions, come between us and God? What do we hold onto tightly, refusing to let go?

Our possessions come in many shapes and forms—it isn't always all about money or physical objects. Perhaps it's our expectations of ourselves or others. Maybe it's our sure and firm conviction: our certainty about things and our tendency to be closed to opposite or alternate views. There are many things we may struggle to give up, but perhaps the greatest is giving up ourselves—taking all we have and spending ourselves and our possessions on others, sharing freely the gifts we have each been blessed with. Whatever our gifts are, they are meant to be used and given to others in service to the Lord. To refuse to share what we have and who we are is turning our back on God.

We need God's wisdom if we are to realize that wealth and possessions are nothing compared to the Love of God and eternity spent with Him in His kingdom. The Book of Wisdom tells us we can find wisdom through prayer.

Realizing that I was only human,
I prayed and was given understanding.
The spirit of Wisdom came to me.
I regarded her more highly than any throne or crown.
Wealth was nothing compared to her. (Wisdom 7:7–11, GNT)

In Hebrews we hear that *"the word of God is living and active, sharper than any two-edged sword…"* (4:12–13, ESV).

God's Word is the ultimate wisdom, with the power to penetrate and transform every heart that receives it.

The rich young man reminds us that we all have an innate hunger for something more, and we know what we are yearning for: the Good News of Jesus. Only I can know what Jesus means to me. Sharing the importance of our loving Lord and Redeemer is doing my part in spreading the good news.

Pope Benedict XVI said it well: "Evangelization is teaching the art of living; showing the path toward happiness through Christ."[23] I see it as learning to live in the light of Christ a bit more every new day we are given, and allowing that light to shine forth for others through our words, our actions, our attitudes, and even our perceptions of those we relate to and come in contact with.

In recent years there has been a movement toward "new evangelization" within the Church. The focus of this approach is on those who once believed and practiced their faith, but at some point became disenchanted with the Church and discontinued any active participation in the practice of faith. But there is nothing new about evangelization.

Personally, I think there might be a danger in trying to rebrand what Jesus Himself instructed us to do: *"…go and make disciples of all nations, baptizing them in the name of the Father and of the Son and of the Holy Spirit…"* (Matthew 28:19).

Indeed, our efforts to evangelize go beyond those who may have never heard the Good News. Our efforts must include those who have chosen to no longer believe. Our efforts must also include all of us who do believe but at times struggle with doubts, questions, with disappointments with our Catholic Church. That is fundamentally what the Church is about.

---

[23] Extract from an address by Joseph Cardinal Ratzinger to catechists and religion teachers on December 12, 2000: "The New Evangelization, Building the Civilization of Love."

That's what happens every time we gather as a community around the table of God's Word and the table of the Eucharist, and every time we receive Christ Himself in Holy Communion. In our communal prayer we reach out to one another, and we support and help one another to grow as committed, loving disciples of Jesus. There we find true and lasting newness in life. There we are given the graces, strength, and courage to offer that very same newness to others.

Evangelization happens when we experience the profound love of Jesus, when we allow Him to touch and move our lives. How we live that experience is what allows others to also experience the presence of our Lord in their lives each day.

> *By this everyone will know that you are my disciples; if you love one another.* (John 13:35, NIV)

Thought for Reflection

How do I carry out my Christian responsibility to share the Good News—a responsibility given to us by Christ Himself?

Do I believe that if I share my own experience of God's great love to another person there is the potential of giving that person new hope, of transforming her or his heart?

Sixteen
Be Joyful in Who You Are

IT IS EASY today (and probably always has been) to forget just who we are as individuals. We live in a fast world, and we think we always have to keep pace and be on top of it all. And we begin to teach our children to do the same at a very young age. We enroll them for preschool as early as age three so they are better prepared to face junior kindergarten at age four, before starting senior kindergarten at five.

Presumably after up to three years of being exposed to a school setting and acclimatized to the process of learning, our young children are finally ready to begin grade one.

I wonder at times if we haven't taught them that learning is a chore, a full-time job, work-intensive—one that you never can get on top of, but simply leading to a continuation of the process toward the next step. In many ways going to school is like playing a sport, any sport: the ultimate objective is to win, period. I am afraid that often our wish to instill in them a thirst to learn gets lost in the process and becomes their first lesson in the competitiveness of life.

A quick search on the web reveals that "Preschool programs provide early childhood education and care for children, and help them develop a range of skills that make them ready to learn when they start school, such as social skills: the ability to empathize and interact successfully with their peer group, and also relate easily to adults."[24]

---

[24]   https://www.child-encyclopedia.com/preschool-programs#what-are-main-functions-preschool-programs

Let's be real, we spend our whole lives trying to develop social skills, learning to care, listen, empathize, and be there for one another. And my experience tells me that young children relate more easily and directly to adults than adults relate to each other. From the youngest age, children let their parents and caregivers know what they need, what they want, and how they feel. Their language may be a challenge at times, but the message is there: honest, sincere, and direct.

Why society wants to rush the process is beyond me. Children need to discover who they are as children before they can ever discover who they are as teens or adults. And that discovery involves play, having fun, learning how to be creative with sticks, stones, and blocks—watching their creation fall apart and learning to rebuild. Such discovery takes whatever time it takes.

As we grow and mature, we progress one grade at a time until we think we are ready for the real world of work and responsibility. Then we begin to learn our job, our trade, and our profession until we are challenged with the prospects of promotion, or get tired and bored with what we are doing. Either way, it leads us toward learning something new, more intense, and different. Pretty soon it's time to retire—and guess what, we've been so busy trying to keep on top of things all our lives that we haven't learned how to live with ourselves, nor what we are to do with all this newfound time.

No matter what our age or educational background is, or the social setting we find ourselves in, the single greatest lesson we can ever learn is that each one of us is, first and foremost, a child of God. And not just any child, but a *beloved* child of God. Unfortunately, many of us never fully come to understand or accept that. For others, though, that comes as one of the gifts of aging.

Knowing that I am God's loved son is what matters most in my life.

I know what it is to experience God's presence in my life.

I know what it is to receive God's mercy and forgiveness—to feel freedom as the weight of guilt from sin, coldness, indifference, pride, and self-reliance is lifted.

I know what it is to feel God's personal and intimate love and tenderness in the sharing of life with Joanne, in the beauty and awe every parent experiences with the gift of children, and in the warmth and affection of little grandchildren tucking their faces snugly into the nape of my neck; then, as they grow older, trusting me enough to share their own life experiences, goals, and accomplishments.

I know the awe of waking to a new morn, hearing the sounds of life and nature, and noticing the beauty of creation. And I know what it is to hear God's whisper in the stillness, calling me back to Him when I fail to recognize these everyday things that He gifts me with in life.

But I also know what it is to feel fearful and isolated when I fail to turn to God.

As God's beloved child, bearing His very image, saved and redeemed by Christ His Son, I have much to be joyful about. Despite my weaknesses, failures, and sins, or perhaps more to the point, precisely because I am a sinner, God continuously calls me to Him in tremendous love, wanting to fill me with inner peace and joy and the assurance that I am His.

In the stillness and quiet of my heart, with full awareness of my shortcomings and sins, I am confident in God's forgiving and unconditional love. And in that love, I believe that in the fullness of God's plan for me, I will become ever more fully whom He created me to be. This allows me to be bold enough to be joyful in who I am.

Joy is not necessarily the absence of suffering; it is the presence of God.[25]

Thought for Reflection:

Life is often heavy and discouraging. What are some of the things that you find joy in?

Do feelings of joy sometime surprise you? What causes you to search for things that give you happiness and a sense of joy?

---

[25] Sam Storms, *Pleasures Evermore: The Life-Changing Power of Enjoying God.* Carol Stream, IL: Tyndale House, 2014.

What might free you from expectations (your own and others') to simply be who you are as a child of God?

I tell you, ask and you will receive; seek and you will find; knock and the door will be opened to you. For everyone who asks, receives; and the one who seeks, finds; and to the one who knocks, the door will be opened. What father among you would hand his son a snake when he asks for a fish? Or hand him a scorpion when he asks for an egg? If you then, who are wicked, know how to give good gifts to your children, how much more will the Father in heaven give the Holy Spirit to those who ask him? (Luke 11:9–13, NABRE)

Thought for Reflection:

What is something in your life right now that you ask from God?

How do you Ask, Seek, and Knock when you pray to God for help or in thanksgiving?

Seventeen
Signs of God's Presence

"Pick up your pallet and walk."

ST. JOHN RECORDS the account of a man who had been lying by the pool of Bethesda, where many people went to be healed. This man had been an invalid for thirty-eight years. When Jesus asked if he wanted to be made well, he replied that he couldn't get into the water on his own. No one helped him, and when he did try, others beat him to it. Jesus said to him: *"Get up! Pick up your pallet, and walk"* (John 5:8, NASB).

Many translations use the word "mat," but I prefer "pallet." There was nothing plush, soft, or cushy about where this man had lain for all those years. Pallet more clearly paints a picture of just how difficult life was for him—an indication that his disability was burdensome. It was a heavy cross for him to bear.

There are times in everyone's life when life gets extremely tough to manage. Maybe it relates to health, or the loss of work or someone you love, or a task that circumstances dictate you have to take care of, but you don't even know where to begin. You feel alone—you feel that you just can't do it on your own, yet there is no one to help you. You turn to God in prayer, but even then, you feel like life has turned upside down and you can't get upright.

There are times in our lives when it is difficult to recognize that God really is with us. We can get discouraged, and might even have doubts that He is listening to our prayer or truly journeying with us.

I have been praying for some of the same individuals for a long time. For some, I pray that they may discover God's invitation to have an intimate relationship with Him. For others, I pray they may be freed from pain, from the anguish of debilitating illnesses, whether physical or emotional. I pray for others who are dying, that they might know God's love and mercy. And I pray for the healing of family relationships.

There are many instances when I do not see God responding to my prayer. There have been instances when after a time, waiting but not seeing God attend to these individuals, I have found myself feeling angry that He has not yet intervened. For you see, I do believe that if I do not pray with the expectation that God will answer, then my prayer is not truly sincere. And I also believe that I can vent my anger directly to God, because more than anything, He wants my prayer to be from my heart. He never wants me to be afraid to express to Him exactly what's going on in my life, including my prayer life.

"Get up! Pick up your pallet and walk" presents a picture of healing, of being set free—a glimpse of the love and compassion of our Lord.

Mathew (16:24), Mark (8:34) and Luke (9:23) each record strikingly similar words spoken by Jesus: "Take up your cross and follow Me." I believe that by referencing the cross, there is an intended harshness in these words. Jesus is making it very clear that if we are to follow Him, our lives will *not* be free of pain and suffering, and there *will be* heavy burdens that we will have to pick up and carry.

Some of the burdens we carry are internal and relate to what's going on in our own lives—to what is happening to us personally, whether physical, emotional, or spiritual in nature. But very often equally heavy burdens are external. They go beyond ourselves and relate to others.

At some point, each of us will experience feelings of helplessness as we watch someone we love curl up in fear or cry out in excruciating pain. It may be an aging parent, a daughter or son, a wife or husband, or a dear friend. Seeing someone we love going through such painful times is often very gut-wrenching, one of those hard encounters we face in life.

We, as individuals and as a society, have a difficult time accepting any serious degree of pain, fear, or suffering. We like our lives to run smoothly. We like to be comfortable in our skin, with good physical, mental, and spiritual health. We fight with all we have to be in control of what happens in our lives, and in the lives of those closest to us. We expect to be comfortable in all of our relationships. Many of us would be willing to go to nearly any length to be personally free of turmoil and suffering or to see someone we love freed from ongoing pain.

Regrettably, no one needs to look very far to see turmoil and suffering. Every one of us has come face to face with sickness and struggles, with great chaos in our own lives or in the life of someone we know. And if you happen not to have encountered such life experiences personally, then a view of the local or global news on any given day will paint clear and bold pictures of violence, inequalities, food and medical deprivations, and discrimination spewed out in a wide variety of ways and against a wide variety of individuals.

The reality is that we are all affected to some degree by what happens to us or around us. No one is exempt. Post-traumatic stress is a reality for so many people, yet despite it being extremely common, it is often overlooked, misdiagnosed, or denied.

Because such hatred, vengeance, intolerance, and abuse of every type imaginable can be viewed in the comfort of our living room, we run the sad risk of becoming immune to what we witness and hear. Even when this sort of "news" comes through a reputable outlet, the sheer repetitive nature of such reports can render the account as just another typical TV show. Our minds may not want to accept what we see or hear, and we tune out. I think history has shown that when any type of event gets repeated often enough, we begin to expect more of the same, and if we as individuals, and society as a whole, are not fully awake and vigilant, even the most horrific examples of violence and hatred can become the norm.

Whether we are the ones going through a terrible ordeal, or the ones accompanying someone who is, the result is the same—the stuff of life can get very heavy and hard to carry. But life goes on, and carry it we must. Thankfully, God in His goodness created us as social beings and fashioned us in His likeness to be caring, attentive, and responsive to one another. If we live our lives as followers of Jesus, we will try our utmost to be there. We will listen, offer comfort, encourage, support, and walk step-in-step with one another. That is discipleship; that is being Christ-like with and for others. That is how we become the hands and feet and voice of God. That is being Church, alive, well, and actively present in this twenty-first century.

So, while Matthew, Mark, and Luke's account of Jesus' words "take up your cross" carry a harsh tone, they also imply the same connotation that we looked at in the words "pick up your pallet and walk": a picture of healing, of being set free, a glimpse of the love and compassion of our Lord.

So again, whether we are carrying our own burden or being there in whatever way we can to help another carry theirs, we can have some surety that God is right there with us, giving us the strength we need at the moment, guiding us and helping us to shoulder the load.

Because pain, suffering, and grief are universal and touch every person, we can learn so much by spending time, alone or with others, reflecting on these difficulties. We can invite God to join in, to lead us in our thoughts and reflections, and to let us know how He is present in all this.

Many commonalities can be observed through the clouds of life that unite us. With nearly every struggle we face:

- emotions such as fear, disillusionment, betrayal, distrust, and/or isolation may build up
- we often experience increased negativity toward nearly every aspect of life as a natural consequence of such feelings
- there may be a real reluctance and even fear of going out where there may be a lot of people or noise—the fear of being exposed to yet another event, occurrence, or trigger
- there might well be a degree of depression, or at the very least fatigue. One gets tired of fighting ever-occurring bouts with the evil that has happened and just won't desist.
- sometime that fatigue turns to the desperation of simply wanting it all to end. A glance at the obituary notices of any given day might well reveal that such desperation can lead to suicide.

But I have also observed that those who strive to live a life of faith and belief in a loving God:

- have an inner strength, courage, and resolve to face, carry, and fight these struggles to the very best of their ability
- have a comfortable reliance on the power of God and the intercession of Mother Mary or a favoured saint
- recognize the need to have someone in whom to place complete trust— someone they can count on to be present; someone wanting to understand, bit by bit, day by day, regardless of the fight or the fear being faced
- desire deeper relationships with family and friends based on mutual trust, acceptance, and respect
- are more prepared to seek help and guidance from a professional, if it's felt needed, with whom they can relate and be open
- need "someplace" to praise and worship God and be nourished by His Word and His Being in Eucharist. For many, this can be a fight on its own, given how the Church itself has been a source of many pains and triggers in how it has dealt (or failed to have dealt) with clergy sexual abuse.

At the beginning of this section, I said that the past number of years have been challenging for me. When the ones whom I love are struggling intensely, it affects me. I experience feelings of helplessness, anxiety, fatigue, discouragement, and even depression as I watch and witness their suffering. I can at times have feelings of anger toward every person and every situation that caused the fear, the burden, the trauma—even toward those who brought about one more trigger.

I often tend to want resolutions, conclusions, reasons, or some kind of explanation to aid my understanding. Always, I am left with open questions: Why? Why? Why? How can people cope with so much? What can I do? What now?

These are some of the things that go on in my physical and emotional being, and there seem to be just as many things going on in my spiritual life.

I've already confessed to you my frequent conversations with God about my anger, and not only about people and events, but at God Himself. At times I try to kid myself into thinking that my prayer is just intense, though pleading, but at the same time I find myself complaining: This has been so long now, Lord, why aren't You giving this or that person a break? Why not give him or her some relief and allow others like me who are healthy to carry their sufferings, even for a little while? If I am not strong enough, then strengthen me, give the other a break and release her or him, at least long enough to regain strength.

There is one question that keeps nudging its way to the forefront: Lord, what is it that You are trying to tell me in all this? What is the takeaway, for me and for others?

God must have some good hearty laughs at how I behave:

- "Wow, isn't he something else; he thinks his timing might be better than Mine!"
- "To him a few years are forever; he can't comprehend that time is time- less to me."
- "He does pray with a sense of expectancy, but he lacks faith."

It's that last one that causes me great pause and reflection. "He lacks faith."

Sacred scripture frequently records Jesus healing physical, emotional, and spiritual sicknesses.

In the very first book of the Bible, we hear God's promise to all of us: *"I am with you and will watch over you wherever you go, and I will bring you back to this land. I will not leave you until I have done what I have promised you"* (Genesis 28:15, NIV).

In Matthew's Gospel, there is the wonderful story of the centurion who tells Jesus about his paralyzed servant. When Jesus offers to go back with him to heal the servant, the centurion humbly says that he is not worthy to have Jesus come to his house, but in faith and trust, tells Jesus that all He has to do is say the word and his servant will be fine. Jesus assures the man, *"Go! Let it be done just as you believed it would"* (Matthew 8:13, NIV). And his servant was healed.

In the very next couple of verses, Jesus is going home with Peter and sees Peter's mother-in-law in bed with a fever. *"He touched her hand, and the fever left her, and she rose and began to serve him"* (Matthew 8:14–15, ESV).

And there's Mark's account of Jairus, believing that Jesus could make his sick daughter better, begging Jesus to go with him and bless her. The story says that Jesus follows Jairus, but on the way to the house, He stops to heal a woman, when someone tells him that the girl is now dead. Turning to Jairus, Jesus tells him to believe in Him and not be afraid. When Jesus enters Jairus's house, He tells everyone that the girl is sleeping. He takes her by the hand and tells her to get up, and she stands up and walks (Mark 5:21–43).

Another story is of a woman who had been bleeding for twelve years. She comes up behind Jesus, confident that if she can just touch his clothing, she will be healed. Jesus turns and tells her, *"…Take heart… your faith has made you well"* (Matthew 9:20–22, ESV).

Jesus revealed the Father's love and mercy through many physical signs, and He gave His disciples the authority to do likewise: *"…whoever believes in me will do the works I have been doing, and they will do even greater things than these…"* (John 14:12, NIV).

This is the awesome gift of healing that we can observe in modern medicine. But it is also the gift and commission the disciples received from Christ. The scripture story about Peter and Aeneas illustrates this. Aeneas was paralyzed and had been confined to bed for eight years. And Peter said to him: *"Aeneas, Jesus Christ heals you. Get up and roll up your mat."* And immediately Aeneas got up (Acts 9:34, NIV).

So, what does all this say to me?

In a nutshell: God is with us always. No matter where we are or what we do, He is there to help us, give us what we need, and forgive us. God doesn't care how we pray or what words we use. He simply wants us to share our lives with Him, and with Him in others. And He wants us to allow Him to share the fullness of His life with us. He waits for us to hunger for Him. Christ showed us that to do that: we need to go to some quiet place, free of outside distractions, and just listen.

In that stillness, He will speak to us. There He will offer us comfort and renew in us a more profound sense of purpose and belonging. He will offer us fresh evidence of His presence in our everyday life: in the sunlight, in the breeze, in the

> God doesn't care how we pray or what words we use. He simply wants us to share our lives with Him, and with Him in others. And He wants us to allow Him to share the fullness of His life with us.

beauty of life and creation, and most amazingly, in the darker, anxious clouds of life. God has shown throughout history His willingness and His desire to heal and make well.

Whoever believes in me will do the works that I do is not simply an invitation from Jesus, but rather His commission to every one of us to do His work in the here and now of our everyday lives.

Here's the kicker: humankind throughout history has repeatedly failed to express real faith in the face of hardship—failed to claim His healing either for ourselves or for others.

I think many of us are reluctant to say "God has healed me!" And we are equally hesitant—even fearful—to say to another, as Peter said to Aeneas, "In the name of Jesus Christ, be healed."

What if that other person is not healed? What if the sickness or situation comes back? We might look foolish, or fear that others will belittle or make fun of us.

Intercessory prayers are very important, not just for the person being prayed for, but also for the one offering the prayers. No matter how badly we want God to grant something in particular, every intercessory prayer should be that God's will be done: in His way, in His perfect time, and for His glory. It takes conviction: courage, trust, and faith.

People who demonstrate both patience and steadfastness in their trust that God will indeed answer their prayers are tremendous sources of inspiration.

I, on the other hand, am impatient, wanting to see results quickly. Not only do I want to see my prayers answered, but I want them answered when and how I think would be best, and in a direct response to how I have asked them.

I profess my belief in God, in the power of prayer, and in the power of the Spirit bestowing all the graces I need to get through the chaotic events of life. But while I am ashamed to admit it, in the pain of watching others—especially loved ones—suffer, my faith is weak. My profession of belief is more knowledge in my head than conviction in my heart. I lack trust in God, and in my impatience, I question and complain to Him.

Under my breath, in the silence of my heart, I claim healing in Jesus' name, but I have not voiced it; I have not allowed anyone to hear it. In that silence, I have not trusted in God's great love and providential care.

Fear can be such an overpowering emotion. It can hinder our ability to model the faith lived and shared by those around us. We all need people in our lives who live their faith and belief in God, who bring witness to God's Word and to His presence in the way they go about their daily routine.

I am grateful to have encountered and known such models of Christianity in my life. They inspire and challenge me to *"live by faith and not by sight"* (2 Corinthians 5:7, CEB), to trust in God regardless of the situation at any given point in time. They have made a powerful impact on my life, and have strengthened my resolve to live one day at a time with deep gratitude for all that has been given to me.

Fear can deafen us to God's call to put our faith into action. It can cripple us and lead us to think that we are incapable of offering any real help. That is not what God whispers to us, for with Him there is no such thing as being helpless or useless to another in time of need. Jesus Christ made His purpose, His commitment to you and me, very clear: *"I have come that they may have life, and have it to the full"* (John 10:10, NIV).

God gives each of us wholeness of life, and we can experience and live that wholeness to the degree that we are willing to believe and accept it.

One final passage that speaks to me, that says it all, that challenges me: *"Stop your doubting, and believe!"* (John 20:27, GNT).

"Lord, I believe; help my unbelief," as recorded by St. Mark (9:24, NKJV), is a prayer to remember.

Thought for Reflection:

God has withheld nothing from me. How do I discern what I need to carry, and what I might be able to let go of?

What holds me back from giving my all to him in complete surrender, trust, and faith-filled conviction?

Who inspires me by the way they carry the weight of their burdens and struggles?

Whom do I know that might benefit from my simply being there today, present, attentive, and caring? How am I doing with that?

Lord Jesus, You love me into wakefulness, and You welcome me into this *New Day*.

Eighteen

You Love Me into Wakefulness

…have pity on me and send Lazarus to dip the tip of his finger in water and cool my tongue… (Luke 16:24)

I GOT UP this morning feeling very unrested and not sure that I wanted to be awake yet. But, being a creature of habit, I did what I usually do. I made myself a coffee and went and sat quietly in my soft comfortable chair.

I contemplated this day and how it might unfold, and I asked God to let me know (very clearly) how I was to serve Him today and what He wanted to tell me. Almost immediately it was like God was saying, "Just let me love you into wakefulness, and I will welcome you to journey with me into this *New Day*."

So, what might be the wakefulness that God desires to love me into today? Well, first of all He wants me to be awake to my breath, to my life, to my immediate surroundings—awake and cognizant of what He has given me *this* day. He wants me to begin today aware of my own life, of the precious gift of my wife and my family, and the health that we do enjoy.

He wants me to remember and be grateful for the security that we enjoy. We have never known what it is to be hungry and without food or clean water to satisfy ourselves. We have never had to live on the street, not knowing how or if we will make it.

He wants me to be conscious of my own free will—the times that I have chosen to follow His lead, even with the swerves and stumbles, and the times I have not. Both choices—following God and not following Him—have each had an impact on others, for the good and the not-so-good.

Our loving God wants me to acknowledge that it all is His gift. But there is far more.

He wants me to be awake to His presence in every single person I encounter, beginning right here at home, acknowledging their dignity by showing them respect and acceptance. He wants me to be especially awake to who they are. Am I prepared to look directly at them and give them my full attention?

And He wants me to be awake to those around me, those I encounter during my day. Based on what they say, or don't say, is there anything that they might appreciate from me? It might be a smile, a friend, a ride, a coffee, or some specific thing that I can help them with. Perhaps they want an opportunity to seek forgiveness, or to forgive someone else. Maybe what they need most at this very moment is the space to be left alone.

Prayer is always a gift that keeps on giving, even if said in silence. I need to recognize the Lazarus in my midst and share what I can—even crumbs, if that's all I can offer. God wants to make me conscious of my tendency to let things slip through my mind so I can do better.

God also wants us to be awake to what is going on in our community, our parish, our city, our country and our world. As tired as I get of hearing the same news stories repeated several times a day, there is a reason it happens. It is hard to offer support of any kind if we don't hear of the need, and I need to hear things repeatedly before they sink in.

We can be very quick to say there is nothing we can do about this or that—it is too big for me; I'm not qualified or able to do what needs to be done; it's beyond my control (there's that word again.) But there are things we can do.

We can contribute to needy causes, no matter how little. We can offer our time and presence in those situations where there is something we can provide. We can offer physical, emotional, and spiritual help to those in need, in simple ordinary ways.

We can listen without any kind of judging. We can shovel snow or cut grass for a neighbour who cannot do it right now. We can offer rides. We can be a friend. We can pray for and with others. Our world is in dire need of constant prayer.

God also wants me to be aware of my own need for Him and for others and what they have to offer me. Although I have all the material stuff I need—and then some—there are still many ways in which I am poor. I need God in my life, and I need the support, encouragement, and friendship of those around me. There is great richness in the crumbs and drops of water that others offer me. I need to know that I can ask, and I need to be humble enough to accept.

I need the graces of the Holy Spirit in everything I think, say, and do. I know my many faults and weaknesses, but I need others to fill me in on those that I do not recognize on my own—those things I do or say robotically at times, without any forethought of how they may be received or interpreted. And knowing them, I know my need for forgiveness from God and from others whom I have hurt.

God wants me to know that He is always eager to transfigure my heart, which is cold and scarlet, and make it white as snow. I should realize that through Him, forgiveness can always be obtained, including the forgiveness I need from others.

Probably most of all, God wants me to be awake to His Love, no matter what situation I find myself in today. I think many of us have this twisted idea that God wants nothing to do with us when we fall from grace—when we sin and err. With that kind of "stinkin' thinkin'" comes the notion that we have to make things right on our own before we can find favour once more with God.

But these are the times when God is most near to us. The times He offers outstretched arms to receive us, to heal us, and to give us the grace and strength to turn our life around. We simply need to allow Him in and accept His love.

God wants me to have my eyes and my heart open to see Him; to notice His mighty works—in the here and now, in my life, in the lives of those around me, and in the world, despite the darkness we may see there. Jesus, our Lord and our Saviour, continues to do marvellous and awesome miracles today, not only all around us; but even more importantly, within each of us.

...God is able to make every blessing of yours overflow for you, so that in every situation you will always have all you need for any good

work. As it is written, "He scatters everywhere and gives to the poor; his righteousness lasts forever."

Now he who supplies seed to the farmer and bread to eat will also supply you with seed and multiply it and enlarge the harvest that results from your righteousness. In every way, you will grow richer and become even more generous, and this will cause others to give thanks to God because of us... (2 Corinthians 9:8–11, ISV)

Thought for Reflection:

What is it that I tend to want to ignore, to close myself off from?

What is God loving me to be awake to today?

Who is God loving me to be awake to love today?

Nineteen

You Welcome Me into This New Day

ST. AUGUSTINE SAID that all of us, made from nothing, tend toward nothing. This is pretty clear when we look at our lives: we are weak, frail creatures. We stumble and we fall so often in life— in physical ways, in emotional ways, and certainly every bit as clearly in spiritual ways.

We tend to lose track of who we are, who God is, and how we stand in our relationship with Him. We tend to think that we are in control of what happens in our own life: what we do, what we think, and who we are. But if we are honest with ourselves, we know our weaknesses, and we know that there are specific temptations we struggle with on an ongoing basis. For example, a weakness may show up in our conversations with others. We may be short and abrupt; we might cut another up, speak negatively about someone, spread gossip, or outright lie about another's words, actions, or character.

We are often so very quick to argue our point that we fail to listen carefully to someone else's opinion. We may even gloat about how right we are, and how foolish the other is to think the way they do.

I suspect many of us find it very easy to judge how someone else behaves or talks, or even how she or he looks and sounds. We tend to think that we can relate better to those who share the same interests and profess the same beliefs as us.

In our world of insecurities, it is often hard to be generous to another, either with our time or in sharing what we have with those who have less. We often think we have to save, save, and save some more… because we don't know what lies ahead for us. What if we lose our job or our ability to work? What if our nest egg isn't enough to sustain us in retirement? What if something major breaks down again? (It's never just one thing at a time!)

And then there is how we care for our bodies. When we feel lonely, or when we are upset, tired, angry, or frustrated, what do we do? I bet our first choice is not to kneel or sit down and thank God for the opportunity to grow.

No, we are more likely inclined to go searching for something we think will satisfy us, even if just for the moment. We might raid the fridge or the cupboard, drink, smoke, or indulge in any number of addictions that might distract us from how we are feeling. So often as our first step we go toward nothing. So where is God in all of this?

Well, first of all, He lets us do what we choose to do. He honours our freedom to exercise our will as we please. We may quickly come back to our senses and go to our God, who is the only source of comfort, of help. Or we may linger in that messiness of self-comfort, fooling and lying to ourselves.

But whenever we are ready to return to God, ready to profess our need for the Holy Spirit to open our hearts to receive all the graces that He wants to shower on us, and ready to confess our sins with openness and honesty, God is always there to receive us. He will never say we were justified in doing wrong. Wrong is always wrong. Evil is always evil. But in His gentleness and eagerness to have us back in relationship with Him, He will say to us what we hear through the prophet Isaiah: *"Come now, let us set things right, says the Lord"* (Isaiah 1:18, NABRE).

God always welcomes us to set things right, to start afresh, as though every moment of the day is the beginning of a new one. He welcomes us to trust Him, to believe in Him, and to follow Him.

Our Lord doesn't just invite us—no, He receives us and welcomes us with a loving embrace. Just as a child runs into his or her parent's arms, so our God gives us a bear hug when we run to Him. He welcomes us to receive, today, all that He gives us—beginning with continued breath, right now in this very second.

Every day God consistently invites us to know just how precious and important we are to Him, to recognize His presence to us at all times—of course at the times of happiness and joy, but even more so when we are bowed down under the weight of fear, sickness, and grief.

We all experience many cloudy days in our lives, and we all have a very real need to listen and look for the various ways that our loving God reveals Himself to us. A child on the street is playing and laughing. New life is born into the family, or to friends. New life is peeking through the soil in spring.

The sun is teasing us through the clouds as they drift aside, even the slightest bit. Someone we care for stops in for a visit or calls at just that moment when we need picking up.

Our God is welcoming. He welcomes anyone and everyone who believes into his family. Jesus always welcomed anyone into His presence wherever he was. He is our example. We should never be shy about welcoming others. Whether it's welcoming friends into our home or visitors into our church, or just saying hello to a stranger on the street, as Christians we should display the welcoming attitude of God.

God in His love and compassion always gives us some glimmer of hope, of joy. We should always be looking for that simple sign that God is with us in the ordinary course and routine of daily life.

Why?

Because He wants us to never doubt that we are his beloved daughter, his beloved son, and He is with us through it all as He welcomes us into every second of this *New Day*.

When they came to Jerusalem, they were welcomed by the church and the apostles and the elders, and they declared all that God had done with them. (Acts 15:4, ESV)

When the crowds learned it, they followed him, and he welcomed them and spoke to them of the kingdom of God and cured those who had need of healing. (Luke 9:11, ESV)

Therefore welcome one another as Christ has welcomed you, for the glory of God. (Romans 15:7, ESV)

Thought for Reflection:

As a baptized Christian, how well do I welcome others into my circle of friends, especially those whom I struggle to get along with?

How well do I welcome and accept what God wants to offer me today, in prayer, through the Sacraments and teachings of the Church, and through those individuals I encounter through the routine of daily life?

Being Witness
and Doing It for Love

Twenty

Being Witness

WHAT DOES IT mean to be a witness?

According to well-known dictionaries, a witness is:

- one who sees an event take place and can testify to what was seen or heard[26]
- "one who has personal knowledge of something"[27]

What are the things of our faith we are witnesses of?

Let's start with the "what."

In faith we have witnessed that Jesus was crucified, died, and on the third day rose from the tomb—that He is not a ghost, but the living Lord. And that is not blind faith. It is faith supported by first-hand accounts, recorded shortly after events happened by people who did see.

In Luke 24:35–48 (NLT), Jesus appears to the disciples, and they are startled and think they are looking at a ghost. He says, *"Peace be with you"* (v. 36). And He questions their fear and their doubts. He reminds them, *"When I was with you before, I told you that everything written about me in the law of Moses and the prophets and in the Psalms must be fulfilled"* (v. 44).

[26] *Oxford Learner's Dictionaries,* "Witness," https://www.oxfordlearnersdictionaries.com/definition/english/witness_1. Paraphrased.

[27] *Merriam-Webster,* "Witness," https://www.merriam-webster.com/dictionary/witness

This is no falsehood. What is written in scripture is the truth: that Christ would suffer and be raised, and that repentance and forgiveness flow through Him, through His name. And Jesus gives them the instruction: *"You are witnesses of all these things"* (v. 48).

St. Luke writes in the Acts of the Apostles of Peter talking to the people of Jerusalem not long after the events of the Crucifixion and Resurrection. *"You killed the author of life, but God raised him from the dead. We are witnesses of this... Repent, then, and turn to God, so that your sins may be wiped out..."* (Acts 3:13–19, NIV).

We know in faith that repentance and the forgiveness of sins go hand in hand, and that forgiveness happens in the name of Jesus Christ. We also know that at times we are frightened; at times we have doubts in our heads, and we sin and fall from grace. St. John tells us that if we sin, Jesus is our *"advocate with the Father."* But he says even more: *"... whoever keeps his word, in him truly the love of God is perfected"* (1 John 2:1, 5a, ESV).

We've heard and read about the God who created all things and made us in His very image and likeness, about Jesus Christ who freely gave the totality of His life to free us from our sins and the bondage of guilt, and about the Holy Spirit, sent by God to enable us who call upon His help to carry on the mission and life that Jesus calls us to.

And we know all that we have heard and read is true because we have personally experienced the presence of God in our lives. Right from our Baptism, God has claimed us as His own. We are His beloved children. When we mess up and hurt ourselves and others through our selfishness and sins, we know that if we go to God with sincere sorrow and with resolve to accept His love and His grace, we will be forgiven and our slates will be wiped clean.

We have experienced, through the sacrament of reconciliation, the relief and joy of forgiveness, of the weight and burden being lifted, of being set free. These are realities that we have experienced. We are true witnesses of God's love, God's compassion, God's mercy.

So how do we witness and live our beliefs?

We can begin by acknowledging our God first thing every morning.

Thank You, God, for the gift of another day—for giving me life and for sustaining my life this day. And thank You for sending us Your Son—as one of us, one we can relate to and come to know.

Thank You, Jesus. By Your life, You show us how to live full lives in service to others. Only through Your example can we know how to be present to one another, accept our differences, listen to one another, and respect and uphold everyone's dignity.

Thank You, Holy Spirit, for giving me the graces I need today. Without Your presence in my life, I cannot show the love, mercy, compassion, or kindness that others deserve and are entitled to see through me.

Lord God, without knowing Your truth, I cannot speak Your truth. Without knowing how You correct me, not out of anger, annoyance, or frustration, but out of love, I cannot offer proper and true guidance to anyone. Without knowing the fullness of Your love, I cannot fully love those You have placed into my life.

Lord, thank You for feeding us with Your Word, and with the very presence of Your body and blood in the Eucharist.

God has given us all we have and all we need to become precisely whom he calls us to be, one *New Day* at a time. We have much to be grateful for, and indeed we are witnesses of all these things.

But in your hearts honor Christ the Lord as holy, always being prepared to make a defense to anyone who asks you for a reason for the hope that is in you; yet do it with gentleness and respect... (1 Peter 3:15, ESV)

Thought for Reflection:

Does how I live my life, how I relate to others, offer hope and encouragement through the power of the Holy Spirit?

Twenty-One
Do It for Love

I ONCE HEARD a story about a Christmas Eve when a young mother was busy wrapping the last packages. She asked her little son to polish her shoes for Christmas Mass the next morning. So off he went.

The little fellow was gone quite a while, but when he returned, he was beaming as he presented the shining shoes to his mother.

"What a perfect shoe shine!" she said, and with that, she gave him a shiny new quarter for working so hard and doing so well.

The next morning, when she was dressing for church, she found something lodged in the toe of her shoe—something tiny, wrapped in a crumpled piece of paper.

Carefully, she opened the tiny package and inside she found the quarter she had given her son for shining her shoes. Written on the crumpled paper in his childish scrawl were the words, "Dear mother, I done it for love!"[28]

We can relate to the mother in the story. We know what it means to prepare for an event, whether it be what to wear, the food to serve, the lesson, test, or presentation to be given, or the game to be psyched up for. It all takes time and effort. It means getting prepared.

In Sacred Scripture, we hear how God responds to His people, that *He did it for love.*

---

[28] Source unknown

The Book of Baruch is filled with hope and encouragement. Jerusalem had been captured and the Jewish people taken into exile. Baruch tells them that God hasn't forsaken them, that their days of mourning are over, and that they can trust in God's love to bring them back as the newly chosen citizens of the kingdom of God, the New Jerusalem (5:1–9).

Today, many people throughout the world continue to be scattered, or even forced from their homeland. Many are fleeing from oppression and injustice, searching for a new place to call home where they might live in peace and harmony.

We are so very blessed to live here, free from many of the problems that so many of our brothers and sisters around the world face. Yet in this story in Baruch, we hear our own story also, for we too are a people on a journey. We too are confronted with the struggles and demands of daily life. Many in our community face economic uncertainty and other life-changing events.

Like the little boy whose mom asked him for help, we too are asked to reach out and help in whatever ways we can, and we are called to *do it for love.*

We want to be good, holy, and helpful people, but at times our selfishness, pride, attitudes, and sins get in the way.

We too can feel like exiles. We may carry baggage of shame, or guilt or anger. Sometimes we wrap ourselves in sorrow. Grief and despair can get us down. We feel inadequate..

John the Baptist echoes the prophet Isaiah and proclaims a baptism of repentance for the forgiveness of sins, to *"prepare the way of the Lord"* (Luke 3:1–6, ESV). In our preparation for the coming of Christ, we need to admit that our paths, our dealings with God and one another, are not always straight and smooth.

At times we can be selfish, unkind, inattentive, and just plain lax in responding to the injustices of society and the needs of those around us. We have many things for which to seek repentance and forgiveness. We need a conversion of heart.

God created us and gave us many wonderful gifts. Sometimes we take them for granted, and sometimes we fail to use them, yet *not only* was He willing to forgive us, but He sent His divine Son as one of us, to live with us and die for us. He has redeemed us, prepared a place in heaven for us, and given us everything we need to get there.

Only God could have such *love,* such *mercy,* and such a *forgiving spirit,* and *He did it for love.*

Do we recognize what God gives us?

Do we look for and see Christ

- in the routine of our daily lives?
- in the joys and wonders we experience?

Do we think about and relate to the suffering of Christ in sickness, pain, and grief?

The Good News proclaimed throughout the New Testament challenges us to take the real events of our everyday lives—all the suffering and pain, all the anxiety and hopelessness, all the joy and peace—and see them as means to recognize the presence of Christ to us.

This is what being a Disciple of Jesus is all about:

- recognizing the presence of Christ in our lives as salvation that has already come, and
- accepting our responsibility to be His presence to others.

God offers us a personal invitation to accept His call to change—a conversion of heart and attitude—so that we may be humble but joyful deliverers of His presence.

The Good News proclaimed throughout the New Testament challenges us to take the real events of our everyday lives—all the suffering and pain, all the anxiety and hopelessness, all the joy and peace— and see them as means to recognize the presence of Christ to us.

Many around us are lonely, isolated by sickness and the stigma of physical or mental challenges; many are grieving, and many are in need. Perhaps we can best prepare the way of the Lord by responding to those who are crying out in the wilderness, and by doing so *for Love*.

God is in charge, and He says to you and me, "If you let Me, I'll move in and I will reveal Myself to others through you."

At precisely the right time, He will come out in our speech, in our actions, and in our decisions if we let him in to begin with, and He will do it all for love.

Thought for Reflection:

God is Love, and all He does is for our good, and He does it all for love. What is God asking me to do today "for love"?

Name one area of your life in which you know God is acting today.

> *If I speak in the tongues of men and of angels, but have not love, I am a noisy gong or a clanging cymbal. And if I have prophetic powers, and understand all mysteries and all knowledge, and if I have all faith, so as to remove mountains, but have not love, I am nothing. If I give away all I have, and if I deliver up my body to be burned, but have not love, I gain nothing.*
>
> *Love is patient and kind; love does not envy or boast; it is not arrogant or rude. It does not insist on its own way; it is not irritable or resentful...* (1 Corinthians 13:1–5, ESV)

Thought for Reflection:

Do the things I say, my actions, and my attitudes reflect love, as God loves me?

Or do they reflect more on my agenda—to be acknowledged and thought well of by others, or to feel better about myself?

Twenty-Two
Lord Please, Just Today

GOD OUR FATHER,
> thank You for the gift of Your Son, Jesus,
> our Lord and our Saviour.
> Lord Jesus, You revealed the Father to all who would listen and learn.
> Through Your Words and deeds,
> You showed Your followers,
> and all would believe,
> the mighty power, depth and completeness of Love.
> You told those who followed not to be afraid, that the Holy Spirit,
> the oneness of Your love and the Father's love,
> would be with them always,
> and that through Your name,
> they would do even greater things
> then what they saw You do.
> Lord, I am Your follower.
> I believe and trust in that same power and love,
> that flows from You and the Father, through the Holy Spirit living in me.
> In Your sacred name, I command the spirits of fear, anger, anxiety,
> pain, sickness,
> and all those spirits that disrupt my life and get between
> You and me, that they be gone; at least for today.

Free me today of all such distractions
that I may come to know ever more fully
the mighty power, depth and completeness of Love,
that You alone can give me.
In that freedom and love, may I carry You
to every person I encounter or even think of;
and refreshed and strengthened in that love,
may I return and ask your help again tomorrow.
All for the praise, glory, and honour of Your holy name.
Amen.
—Bob

Twenty-Three
The Journey

LIFE, WITH ALL its wonders, joys, and celebrations, together with all its chaos, sadness, and tragedies, is a journey—our journey.

Throughout each of our life journeys, we all make many, many observations. Nature, birds, and animals of every kind, people near and far, and every event or experience has something to teach us. Hopefully, we learn some new element of what our loving Lord is offering to us in everything we experience and observe.

Some of what we observe may at first glance seem rather trivial, but nothing is insignificant in what God has in store for us, in what He wants to instill in us. All of life has the capability of reshaping our attitudes and behaviours.

Every experience, joyful or sorrowful, can refocus our outlooks on life, enhance our appreciation, and deeply enrich our beliefs and our faith in God.

I am grateful to one of our granddaughters for allowing me to share with you a school project she recently completed. I invite you to reflect slowly and often on the following photos and reflections, which in my mind express far better than I could the riches and inspirations that we can glean, not only from our own life journey, but from that of others, young and old, and all life.

The Journey (Adventure Photography)

To me, this photo shows *The Journey* of life. The field and grass symbolize how we are constantly growing just like nature. Our families are the seed that helps us start to grow.

The experiences we have teach us important lessons, just like how rain and sunshine help the crops grow. The rocks show that the path isn't always smooth. Everyone has bad rocky days that made us feel like a big rock was on our shoulders, or a day where we feel small like a pebble.

To me, the side of the barn shows the things in our lives that will never change. After a storm the building may need to be repaired, just like the relationships we have with the people around us may need a bit of repairing sometimes. That's why I love this photo.

The Setting Sun (Landscape Photography)

I called this photo *The Setting Sun* because sometimes great experiences in our life come to an end. This reminds me of the quote by Dr. Seuss, "Don't cry because it's over, smile because it happened."

This photo also shows that even in dark times there will always be light shining through. The sun leaves and it's night, but there can still be light.

In this pandemic, a lot of people have extra time on their hands and are using that time to share their talents online or help get things for people who shouldn't be going out. There will always be light through the darkness. You just have to look for it, like in this photo.

Morning Glory (Pet Photography)

I titled this photo *Morning Glory* because my dog Holly is always very floppy and tired in the morning and when I took this photo it was no different. She can always make you smile.

Each morning when I get her up, she always gives me a big hug and it's a great way to start each day. She is still a puppy and can be a little goofy sometimes. Even if you're not having the greatest day, she can make you laugh and forget all your worries. She truly is a Morning Glory.

When he passes me, I cannot see him;
when he goes by, I cannot perceive him. (Job 9:11)

Thought for Reflection:

How attentive am I to the presence of the Lord in the everyday goings-on in my life?

Do I look for God in what surrounds me, in the perhaps too rare moments of silence and stillness that are often so hard to face, in the beauty of sunshine, clouds, rain, rocks, birds, chipmunks... all of creation that we so often take for granted?

Do I see and welcome God in those I come in contact with, especially in those I find hard to spend time with?

Twenty-Four
Choosing the Right Path

I RECENTLY HEARD a story about an older couple who had just moved into a well-established suburb of a major city. A few days after moving in, the woman was by the window admiring their backyard and she said to her husband: "Look at the clothes hanging on that line in our neighbour's yard. They don't look very clean to me." The following week she saw the same sight: a line of clothes that didn't look washed at all. She told her husband again, adding, "Maybe I should talk to them and give them some suggestions."

The next week she looked out again. Excitedly she looked at her husband and said, "Look at that! Their clothes are dazzling white and the colours are brilliant. I wonder what happened."

Her husband replied, "Yes, I know. I was up early this morning. I washed our windows and I noticed right away how clean their clothes were."

There are many times in life when our vision is distorted and often completely blinded by our outlook on life, the lens through which we look.

I think most of us have at some point in life gotten the wrong impression of someone, maybe just judging by what we saw or heard—or what we *think* we have seen or heard. We may even hold a wrong impression of God, a wrong impression of who we think He is, who we think He ought to be, or how we look at Him, His life, and His mission.

If we take a serious and honest look at our own lives, I believe many of us would have to admit that we very frequently get a wrong impression of ourselves.

I have made many mistakes in my life, but those mistakes don't define me as a total failure. I struggled throughout high school, but that didn't mean I was dumb. I make many slip-ups in my relationships, but that doesn't negate my intentions and desires to be the best I can be. I know I am a sinner, but that doesn't mean God couldn't possibly care for me, or that I am doomed to damnation.

Our perceptions about others, about ourselves, about life or God, can reflect our mood at any particular moment in time. Those perceptions generally say more about ourselves than anyone else. Those thoughts and feelings may be expressions of dissatisfaction, distrust, deep hurt, or guilt. They often reflect something we have experienced, decisions we have made and things we have or have not done.

Things we do or don't do generally come about through choices and decisions we make, and there are plenty of decisions that have to be made in life. Some decisions involve others, and are best if they can be made jointly when appropriate and possible. With other decisions, we're on our own, or very often think we are.

Hopefully, most of our decisions are well thought out and we are fully aware of what we intend to do. But there are some decisions we make to which we give little (if any) thought. Some of the things we do or say, or even prejudices we hold, come from habits we've developed over time. Far too often, habits that are allowed to continue unchecked become routine. Sin is generally a conscious decision to turn our backs on God or one another. Some consequences flow from the decisions that we make into the directions we take, further influencing the subsequent choices we make in life.

Some of those consequences are positive in nature, both to ourselves and to others. But some of our choices carry negative consequences and can be quite destructive in nature. For example, if I am angry over what someone has said about me or done to me, and I then seek revenge and begin to gossip or spread falsehoods against that person, that can be extremely destructive to that individual's image, or even to that person's character or relationships with others. And it doesn't matter if mine was a conscious, well-thought-out choice or simply an instantaneous reaction to strike back.

The single most important and serious choice we have centres around what we are going to do with our lives. How do I want to spend my life? What do I hope to be able to do for myself and others? What would I be good at and what can I offer?

Some consider their future in terms of having a job. Others think in terms of having a career. Others strive to discern what specific vocation they may have a calling to. Often, we tend to think they all mean the same thing, that we can pick whichever word we want: job or career or vocation. However, each of these words has its own meaning, and while there may be overlapping connotations, there is a fairly clear distinction between them.

A job generally refers to what one does to earn a living, one day at a time, whereas career refers to having a long-term goal—an occupation one chooses to pursue over the course of one's life, requiring formal training or education, and offering opportunities for progress and promotion.

Vocation, on the other hand, implies an inner prompting toward a broader purpose in life to which one can apply his or her gifts, abilities, passions, and dreams. There are many different callings that a person may be prompted to or interested in, but God calls each one of us to a specific state of life, to a particular vocation.

The Church says that every baptized believer has the vocation to imitate Christ, to follow the will of God. Focusing and living our lives according to God's desire for us is our first vocation, and the way we get to heaven. We can do this in many ways; the most common would be through marriage, religious life, the priesthood, or single life. They are all vocations to which God calls us.

We may like to think we know what God's will is for us, but life and our human mind and will tend to interpret God's call in a way that suits us best or even puts us in a "good light" in the eyes of others.

To come to know what way of life God is calling us to takes effort; it takes discernment. Effort and discernment involve making time every day to ask God in humble prayer to speak clearly to us, and in the silence of our hearts, we need to listen. This is how we come to understand how God wants us to re-spond to what is going on in the world around us. It is through this process of prayer and discernment that we begin to discover how the Holy Spirit is moving within us, what direction and action God is moving us toward, and how God is missioning us. Vocation is the meaningful work through which God uses us to serve others.

If we tap into our faith, we won't have to be alone in making any of our decisions. Sometimes it is precisely the consequences of our choices or decisions that bring us face-to-face with God. At other times we struggle to work through the pros and cons of various options. And at times it is our desire to be guided by the Holy Spirit so that the decisions we make will help steer and direct our lives, and help us align our wills to God's will.

We have a loving, caring, compassionate Father who knows exactly what we need and what is best for us. He knows what we ought to do, what we'd do better to avoid, and what we should not do.

Scripture gives us many sources of guidance in how we make our choices and decisions, and gives us a certainty that if we trust and rely on God, our way forward will come into focus and we won't be needlessly bumping around in the dark.

Prayer and reflection on God's Word can shed light and direction on our discernment process.

Trust in the Lord with all your heart, and do not lean on your own understanding. In all your ways acknowledge him, and he will make straight your paths. (Proverbs 3:5–6, ESV)

We may not realize or admit it, but everyone needs God's graces and the guidance of the Holy Spirit to know and choose the right path, the right way in which we can most fully do what God created and fashioned us to do.

I have been so very richly blessed in my life. God made it very clear to me that my journey toward Him in eternity was to be through the sacrament of marriage, and that I was to offer myself as fully and completely as I possibly could to Joanne. God brought us together. He formed our partnership.

And it is God who has sustained us through these fifty-five years. God blessed us with three children, then eight grandchildren.

Being a husband, a father, and a grandfather is my vocation.

But God places no limit on how He blesses us, nor on whom He places before us. And God never limits the grace and strength that He gives us to follow His will.

Earlier in this book, I mentioned that I am a permanent deacon. I also told you that I fought the repeated invitations even to simply think and pray about it. But God kept whispering, nudging me through Joanne, who encouraged me to listen to what God was inviting me to, so I would recognize how He was asking me to serve Him and His people. And she accompanied me through every step of the process toward ordination.

What a blessing it has been to witness the faces of people listening to and receiving Jesus in Word and in the Eucharist. And what a blessing it has been to see God's people seeking His mercy and His guidance, and to see them reaching out in service to others. Faith, belief, and trust in God are never realized on one's own, but rather through the accompaniment and support of one another.

We have all heard and can all relate to the parable found in the Gospel of St. Matthew (7:5, NIV): *"first take the plank out of your own eye, and then you will see clearly to remove the speck from your brother's eye."*

To me, Jesus is clearly saying, "Bob, you have no right to judge anyone else; you are no better or worse than they. At times you can see clearly; at times you are blind to my presence right in front of you. Your sight is often blurred by your thoughts, your actions, and your emotions. At times you have tunnel vision."

Yes, that plank in my eye affects how I see, receive, and accept others. But it also affects how I see, receive, and accept myself. Let me offer a couple of examples.

Joanne and I have had our struggles throughout our marriage, and I own many of those struggles. Rather than focusing on what was coming my way, listening attentively, and accepting what I was hearing, I prioritized how I felt. The planks in my eye were selfishness and self-centeredness. I would build a wall of self-defence and even control.

Another example can be seen in how I kept fighting God's calling me to the diaconate. I didn't think I could do it; I wasn't good enough, and I didn't have the knowledge, talent, or ability. The plank in my eye was my "I." I focused on myself and on what I thought I couldn't do, rather than on God and what God could do with me and through me if I let Him.

My very ability to make good choices is reliant not so much on my talents or my strengths, but on my willingness and openness to let God do what God wants to do with and through the gifts He has given to me.

The right path is the path God set for us even before we were born. Choosing the right path depends firstly on going to God, talking to God, sharing with Him our dreams and aspirations, and seeking His grace and guidance. And if we draw a blank on having dreams and aspirations, we need to ask God to fill that void and to help us be attentive to His urgings for us.

Then we have to respond.

Our response to God can go in either direction: toward or away, accepting or rejecting. God gave us the freedom to exercise our wills as we choose, and He will never take control of our will or the decisions we make.

Frankly, some of the decisions we make are quite frivolous and immaterial. Some of them can lead us down a bleak, dark, and even destructive path that leads to emptiness and loneliness. Other decisions can draw us very close to God, to others, to a richness and fullness of life, to joy and satisfaction.

How we exercise our will, the choices we make to follow God's blueprint or to pursue our own, set out the pathway of our lives. Our choices can either shed light or cast a cloud. They can determine how we experience every new moment, every *New Day.*

No eye has seen,
   no ear has heard,
   and no mind has imagined
   the things that God has prepared
   for those who love him. *(1 Corinthians 2:9, ISV)*

It is never a single once and for all decision that leads us in the right direction. Every day, every hour, and even every moment of life calls us to make a choice. Do I eat now? What do I eat? Do I want to go through that bother now? Maybe I should order take-out? From where? These are some of the simpler, non-consequential choices we face.

We can feel weighed down by stressful choices that can carry great consequences. Do I stop what I am doing to help someone in need, or is my agenda more pressing? Do I turn the other cheek when someone hurts me, or do I strike back?

Do I speak what I know to be the truth when others gossip, make false accusations, or tell off-colour jokes or stories, or do I sit on the fence and go along with what's happening?

Do I continue to do things I know I should not do and try to fight personal struggles that I can't seem to shake, or do I seek help from a trusted friend, a professional, or God?

Do I try to do things on my own, and then perhaps go to God when what I try doesn't work, or do I go to God first and seek His grace and help?

What do the words from 1 Corinthians 2:9 quoted above say to me about the choices I make? There have been many books and reflections around this topic of choosing the right path for our life, of discerning how to live in a way that gives God glory and honour in how we serve Him and those around us.

Pope Francis has talked about discernment and the process of discerning God's will. He put it very clearly and very bluntly: "Essentially, it is a matter of recognizing the road travelled by God, who emptied himself, who humbled himself unto death on the Cross. Self-abasement, humility and also humiliation: this is the way, the road of Jesus Christ."[29]

A few years later, he talked about how we go about discerning what God wants of us. He said: "Ask the Lord for the grace to be well aware of what is happening in our hearts, what we prefer doing, that is to say, what touches me most: whether it is the Spirit of God, which leads me to the service of others, or the spirit of the world that roams within me, in my closure, in my selfishness, in so many other things. Yes, let us ask for the grace to know what is happening in our hearts."[30]

Reading and meditating on Sacred Scripture is good for the soul, and it can help bring focus and clarity to the mind and heart. Scripture reveals to us God's love, compassion, and mercy. It can lead to a profound conversation with God—real prayer, if we give ourselves space, time, and quiet.

[29] Holy Mass, Santa Marta, January 7, 2014. https://www.popefrancishomilies.com/home
[30] Holy Mass, Santa Marta, January 7, 2016. https://www.popefrancishomilies.com/home

The Gospels in particular show us the fullness of God's love in the person of Jesus. Jesus's life, words, and actions reveal God's love, compassion, and mercy in concrete and relatable terms.

Jesus draws us toward the Father. He freely and totally gave Himself to save humankind from itself. Reflecting on His life and Word can guide us in discerning how we can live in accord with the will of God.

One passage that comes immediately to mind is what Jesus spoke as He begin the Sermon on the Mount: the Beatitudes.

When Jesus saw the crowds, he went up on the mountain. After he was seated, his disciples gathered around him. Then he began to teach them as follows:

"Blessed are the poor in spirit, for theirs is the kingdom of heaven.

"Blessed are those who mourn, for they will be comforted.

"Blessed are the meek, for they will inherit the earth.

"Blessed are those who hunger and thirst for justice, for they will have their fill.

"Blessed are the merciful, for they will obtain mercy.

"Blessed are the pure of heart, for they will see God.

"Blessed are the peacemakers, for they will be called children of God.

"Blessed are those who are persecuted in the cause of justice, for theirs is the kingdom of heaven.

"Blessed are you when people insult you and persecute you and utter all kinds of calumnies against you for my sake. Rejoice and be glad, for your reward will be great in heaven. In the same manner, they persecuted the prophets who preceded you." (Matthew 5:1–12, NCB)

Thought for Reflection:

What do the Beatitudes say to me about choosing the right path?

How might I relate these words of instruction from Jesus to the words quoted earlier from the Holy Father, Pope Francis?

Twenty-Five

Rejoice and Be Glad, for We Are Promised a New Day in the Kingdom

THE PASSION, CRUCIFIXION, Resurrection, and Ascension of the Lord are fundamental, principal celebrations for all who believe in Christ Jesus.

Every year during Lent we recall and reflect on Our Lord's journey to Calvary, culminating in His suffering and death on the cross to free us from bondage and offer us redemption.

On Easter Sunday, the great sign of our faith as Christians, Christ has risen from the tomb. He has conquered death and lives forever, and offers all who believe in Him the same.

In John 14:2–3 (NIV) we hear: *"My Father's house has many rooms; if that were not so, would I have told you that I am going there to prepare a place for you? And if I go and prepare a place for you, I will come back and take you to be with me so that you also may be where I am."*

So great is this event that Easter Sunday marks only the beginning of the special season in which we continue to celebrate Christ's resurrection. For the following six weeks, we will hear and read of the many appearances Jesus made to His disciples, the times when the Risen Lord walked and talked with them. Having Jesus back again was a joy beyond anything they thought possible.

But their joy would be interrupted again when Jesus returned to His Father at His ascension into heaven. Even in that tremendous sign of God's power and love, His disciples couldn't comprehend what was happening. To them, once again Jesus was taken *"from their sight"* (Acts 1:9, NIV), and we are told they were left *"looking up toward heaven"* (Acts 1:11, ISV).

Christ had established an intimate friendship with them. They didn't want that special time to come to an end. They didn't want to say goodbye to their friend yet again.

We're told *"men in white robes"* (Acts 1:10, ISV) refocused them and brought them back to the task Christ had entrusted to them. They knew that the profound union they had with Christ would last forever. They knew that this was a *New Day* for them.

From Acts 1:6–11 (ISV), we can see that the Apostles know something extraordinary is happening. They ask Jesus,

> *"...is this the time when you will restore the kingdom to Israel?" He answered them, "It isn't for you to know what times or periods the Father has fixed by his own authority. But you'll receive power when the Holy Spirit comes on you, and you'll be my witnesses in Jerusalem, in all Judea and Samaria, and to the ends of the earth."*

In Ephesians 1:17–23, we read that St. Paul is telling the early church of Ephesus that Christ has given a special grace to every person: to apostles, prophets, evangelists, pastors, and teachers. Every one of us has a role, individually and collectively, in the building up of the body of Christ.

As Jesus ascended to the Father, He entrusted his mission to us. He promised to be with us whenever and wherever two or three gather in His name. And He promised to leave us with the Holy Spirit, who would guide us and fill us with His power.

The Ascension of the Lord began a coming-of-age for the early Church. The focus of faith shifted from the presence of Christ in His own body (or His resurrected body), to the presence of Christ in those who believe.

It means that we who believe become His mouth for preaching, His hands for healing, His eyes for seeing, His feet for walking, and His heart wide open to receive and forgive.

In Mark's Gospel, Jesus gives that very role to the apostles: *"Go into all the world and preach the gospel to the whole creation"* (16:15–20, RSVCE).

St. Mark says that certain signs will identify those who believe. By using the name of Jesus, they will cast out evil; they will also communicate in new languages, be protected from harm, and lay hands on the sick and heal them.

We may think these are responsibilities reserved for confessors, doctors, or emergency responders, but Jesus assigned these roles to you, to me, and to all who believe and are baptized. These are the signs of a maturing in faith, of an evangelizing Church.

We have many ideas of what the Church is, and even more of what we think it ought to be. A quiet place to gather and pray, to be nourished by God's Word, and by the Body and Blood of Jesus. It's a place where we can be forgiven in the Sacrament of Reconciliation, supported and offered guidance in our struggles, consoled in our grieving, and offered temporal assistance in our needs.

The Church is also a great challenger. You and I have not yet reached our potential. It is our life journey that moves us toward becoming all God created us to be.

It has been said that Church must comfort the disturbed, but it must also disturb the comfortable.

Our mission as a Church, as Christians, is to actively offer hope. Students fear their future. Families face great struggles. Married couples question their commitment to one another.

Priests and religious have their struggles. Single people face a society tempting them on many fronts. Many feel isolated. Increasing numbers feel alone and misunderstood due to mental illness, race, language, religious beliefs, or anything else that we see and point to as different. Those with an addiction of any kind are often unhelped and untreated.

Every day of our lives, we are presented with opportunities to be witnesses to Jesus and to bring His presence to the world. But we can only do so when our hearts are open to respond and we are willing to listen, willing to accept without judgement, and willing to freely offer support and encouragement.

As baptized Christians, we have a role in God's plan of salvation, and a responsibility to let people know they are valued, loved, and important to God. We need to assure them that *in Jesus,* everything is possible.

Great healings and miracles take root through simple acts of kindness, gentleness, and patience. God reveals Himself in the here and now of life. Miracles happen in the moment.

The Ascension of Jesus Christ calls us to change our attitude. We no longer come to church and follow the teachings of Jesus because that is what we should do as Catholics, but rather because we deeply want that intimate friendship with Jesus, and we are grateful for the inheritance He set out for us with the Father for all eternity.

In his Apostolic Exhortation "Rejoice and Be Glad," Pope Francis puts it this way: "We go from being an *'I have to'* people to an *'I get to'* people."

Our faith should never be an exercise of drudgery and routine, but one of joy and excitement in who we are as Catholic Christians; for in His ascension Jesus has opened the way for our ascension into our heavenly home.

Let us rejoice and be glad, for we are promised a new day in the Kingdom, and indeed that makes this day a *New Day!*

Thought for Reflection:

What can I truly rejoice and be glad about in my life?

Name one time, one experience, or one aspect of your life that brings you closest to God and brings you great joy. Be precise; take time to reflect on it, allow yourself to feel that joy once more, and be grateful.

Life Struggles:
A Test of Faith or an Invitation to Encounter the Presence of God

Twenty-Six

2020–2022: Years of Questioning

By your endurance you will gain your lives. (Luke 21:19, ESV)

AS I WRITE this, the world, including Canada and every other country, is in the throes of COVID-19, which poses a major health threat to everyone regardless of one's gender, colour, religion, age, place of habitation, or any other human characteristic.

COVID-19 is a new illness that can affect one's lungs and airways. It's caused by a virus called coronavirus. The typical symptoms of this virus are a cough, fatigue, high temperature, and shortness of breath, often showing as run-of-the-mill flu-like symptoms.

This fatal disease originated in Wuhan, China in or around November 2019. It spread like wildfire and on January 25, 2020, the World Health Organization declared it to be a worldwide pandemic. As of March 24, 196 countries and territories around the world reported a total of 392,336 confirmed cases and a death toll of 17,147. On April 5 those numbers jumped to over 1,250,000 cases and 68,000 deaths. As I wrote this less than six months later (October 1, 2020), those figures had leaped to over 34,000,000 cases and over 1,000,000 deaths, an increase of three million and forty thousand respectively in just the last eleven days.

By early November, these numbers were increasing every day, and many countries had not yet seen the peak of the first round of this pandemic, let alone any of the subsequent waves.

This was a public health crisis like none before. Many "firsts" were introduced and experienced. The only international travel that was originally entertained was to bring citizens stranded in foreign countries back to their respective homelands. Airspace and airports around the world were under lockdown. International borders were being closed. Here in Canada, interprovince travel was restricted to what was deemed essential only. Every non-essential business across the country was ordered to close. In time, slowly and incrementally they were allowed to re-open with strict health regulations in place to protect workers and the public. Any individual who had symptoms, or who had been in contact with someone confirmed to have COVID-19, and for the longest time, anyone returning to Canada, had to self-isolate for a specified period of time, and anyone outside of their home had to maintain a social distancing of two meters. Public gatherings were limited in size, ranging from two individuals to fifty. In many places, failure to observe these precautionary measures would incur fines and/or imprisonment. These remain scary times.

Across this country, and around the globe, places of worship were ordered closed. Christians of every faith were unable to gather as a community for the great celebrations of Holy Week and the triumphant Easter celebration of the Resurrection of Christ. Churches, mosques, and synagogues all responded creatively, allowing their faithful to watch their respective celebrations virtually, which helped to provide us with a sense of connection with our spiritual community.

Even years later, we are being told in no uncertain terms that this virus is still with us and that we must remain vigilant in respecting and maintaining all public health guidelines. Canada eventually entered a four-stage approach to re-opening. While several countries found themselves in a similar situation, many others were reporting record high numbers of new cases.

It wasn't long before Ontario and many other places in Canada and other countries began to see a substantial surge in new case numbers. The next school year began with trepidation and great concern that new cases would balloon quickly. When fall and colder weather approached, people were drawn more and more to indoor activities, which presented a higher risk of spreading the virus. Add into the mix the fear that the typical flu season would weaken our immune systems and leave us even more susceptible to COVID-19.

It can be quite easy to become obsessed with the continual TV coverage of this pandemic, needing to hear the very latest news releases and the freshest data. It is a serious matter, and everyone needs to be aware of what is happening in the world and their country, but particularly in their city or community. The speed at which this pandemic continues to multiply, and the number of people who are dying from this disease is mind-blowing. If we allow ourselves to become glued to whatever media source we use and observe this topic primarily, we run the risk of wearing down our well-being. The data is very depressing, stressing the worst-case scenarios: self-isolation, people in hospitals dying all alone because not even family members are permitted to be with them in their last days and moments of life.

What are we to make of this in terms of our faith and spiritual growth?

Several things flash to mind. The world has been in a downward spiral toward secularism for some time. People have shifted their attitudes, and are subtly guided and led to relativism. We want to control our own way of life. We have become accustomed to do what we want, and go where we want, whenever we want. In so many ways, many people have become quite self-absorbed.

We are caring and giving people, but too often we care and give from a distance. It's far easier to write a cheque than to offer ourselves and our time in personal service to others. So much of our communication today is via texting, email, or any of the various other methods of "social media," whether with friends, distant relations, or even with family sitting in the same room. In many ways we are a faceless society, choosing to deal with one another from a distance.

Today, in the environment that we are in, even with social distancing and self-isolation we are more mentally and emotionally connected with people from all over the world than we may have been with neighbours only months ago.

The lightning progression of this pandemic has highlighted a serious lack in our health care system here in western society, and far more so in many countries around the globe. But we see countries and political parties working together for the common good of all. In various ways, people are expressing tremendous gratitude for the great work and many hours put in by all health professionals, and the many others who continue to provide the essential needs of society. There is a vast range of these essential workers: those who stock the shelves of our grocery stores, law enforcement officers, ambulance drivers, paramedics, nurses, doctors, cleaners, social workers and psychiatrists, public transit drivers, municipal waste management control, garbage collectors, spiritual care providers, and many—many—more.

Isn't it funny? The bigger the crisis, the more we realize that we are all the same and need one another to survive. Once that sinks in, we begin to look out for one another in ways, places, and times that are best for everyone. The world needs prayer—from you and me.

This is a period like none the vast majority of us have ever before seen. We have had to come to terms with new terminology: social distancing, self-isolation and self-quarantine, lockdown, flattening the curve; all initially suggested and all ultimately mandated, across this great nation and in most countries around the world.

We have had to learn how to do things differently. We go out only for groceries, medical supplies or other absolute necessities. We learn to celebrate birthdays or other special occasions from a distance. We still cannot hug our loved ones unless we live under the same roof, or are part of the same small "bubble."

As Catholic Christians, we went months being unable to participate in the celebration of the Holy Eucharist or any other Sacrament within the walls of our churches. While we were able to join in prayer and watch Mass and other devotionals, televised or streamed, right in our own homes, we were not able to receive Jesus in Eucharist. We could receive Him spiritually into our hearts through prayer, in viewing Mass on our home screens… but that is never the same.

When places of worship here in Ontario, Canada were eventually allowed to re-open, attendance was limited to thirty percent capacity. Public health precautions had to be in place, including social distancing and the use of facial masks.

I think in nearly everything, our social distancing has united us. We have come to know that no one is alone in this, and we all need one another. The same holds true in our spiritual lives.

For me and for many, the very fact that we were not able to worship communally, that we could not receive the Body and Blood of Jesus in Holy Communion, highlighted just how important faith and worship are in our lives. We miss and truly hunger for what we may well have taken for granted—all that we had, and how we could celebrate previously. It has left us with an intense longing to get back to church, a deep spiritual thirst for the sacraments and to receive Jesus fully and physically once again. The Bread of Life not only nourishes us but sustains us through our journey of life.

On top of all of this, there seems to be constant turmoil in our world: people against people, nations against nations, and democracies threatened by autocratic dictators. There have been far too many scenes of violence, hatred, and bloodshed, as seen in Syria and Afghanistan in the last few years.

It is now February, 2022, and the entire world is watching as many are being killed in an attempted military takeover of Ukraine by Russian forces, with millions of Ukrainian women and children forced to flee and find refuge in neighbouring countries, while their husbands, sons, brothers, and fathers remain to fight and try to retain their homeland. The ever-present threat of chemical or even nuclear attacks is being used to prevent intervention by other nations for fear of escalation to a third world war.

Many other major issues are of tremendous concern to the world and all its people. A few of the more pressing problems include climate change; ending poverty around the world, urban and rural alike; "post-pandemic" economic recovery and the balancing act of trying to stimulate the economy while at the same time trying to control inflation; gender equality; accommodating and caring for over twenty-six million refugees (half being children); the inequality of peoples and inequitable distribution of income, food, housing, even medical supplies (eg. coronavirus vaccines). People all around the world face overwhelming challenges.

We have also seen a new, widespread call to end racial discrimination and brutality, in this country and around the world. Thousands have gathered in protest, despite the dangers associated with COVID-19, in solidarity and support of our black and indigenous brothers and sisters. And we are witnessing a tighter, more unified stance of free, democratic countries around the world against repressive tyrannical despots.

In this period of tremendous despair, fear, and isolation, we can perhaps better relate to how the apostles must have felt after Jesus was crucified, or perhaps even directly to the torment Jesus endured on His way to the Cross.

What are we learning in this?

I see our lives as Christians as somewhat like a finely knitted quilt. Joy and sorrow, tears and laughter, comfort and pain, noise and quiet, tranquility and turmoil are all finely and proportionately interwoven into all of our lives here on earth, portraying a photo or mosaic of both who we are and who we are capable of being.

Fr. Mike Schmitz, an American priest and author, said: "Jesus shows us His wounds so that we won't be afraid to show Him ours."[31] St. Thomas More described tribulation as "a gift from God—one that He especially gives to His special friends."[32]

No one ever said it would be easy to be God's friend, and at times we may well feel like saying, "Lord, this is close enough for now." Perhaps the pain we feel—the suffering we see and hear about throughout the world—ought to be a wake-up call, a call to a newness of heart, a new freshness, not only to faith and our belief in God, but to a new appreciation and excitement about the whole of life.

We are experiencing events that are extreme in so many ways. I suspect most of us are fearful of what is yet to come in the following months and perhaps even years.

As of April, 2022, COVID-19 has taken the lives of over six million people around the world and within our own communities—perhaps under our own roofs—and inevitably there will be more, as many people in many countries around the world have still not been vaccinated, due to a wide inequity in the distribution of vaccines.

---

[31] Quoted at https://www.facebook.com/youngcatholicprofessionals/photos/a.213 8942176122425/5227787540571191/. Accessed April 5, 2023.
[32] Quoted at http://www.catholictradition.org/Saints/saintly-quotes1.htm. Accessed April 5, 2023.

Governments, health organizations, and medical professionals warn that multiple new waves are likely to follow.

Life, which we have enjoyed and, yes, taken for granted, is up in the air and we are left in dreadful wonderment of what lies ahead.

Everyone is at some stage along the path toward the realization that we are not able to exercise the "control" we so often thought we had over our own lives—that life, as we have known and celebrated it, may never be quite the same again.

What we can strive to do is unite our fears, our pains, and our sufferings to those of Jesus. We don't have to carry them or worry about them on our own. We carry this cross, like so many other crosses, and we each walk our own stations, but we can express it all to God our Father, just as Christ did. We too can cry out as we journey through our Garden of Gethsemane: "Lord, it would be great if You let this pass; we would all be very grateful, yet not as we want, but according to Your will."

Or we may even have a stronger, blunter cry, like how Jesus cried out while hanging on the cross that He carried for us: "Father, why have you left us in this mess? Where are you in all this? Please, God, help us!"

When the difficult time is all behind us, whenever that ends up being, I pray that we will have learned to lean on our God, to allow Him to help us shoulder what has to be shouldered, to surrender more and more to do His will, to be there for one another, to express our gratitude and to truly rejoice and be glad in the depths of our being for the opportunities given to us each day. Until that time comes, patience and perseverance in faith will help us face all these events as they continue to cast a cloud over our lives.

There may be times when we feel frozen, numbed by pain, loss, grief, or any number of things that may be going on in our lives. But with conscious awareness and effort, we can choose to see and choose to acknowledge God moving in our lives and in our surroundings.

In prayer and belief, we can trust, depend on, and recognize that our loving God is with us always. He will help us carry our pallets, and in the Truth and Light of His presence, we can right now, at this very moment, enter into a *New Day.*

God bless.

Thought for Reflection:

On the cross, Jesus was lifted high and pierced with a soldier's sword,
to heal us.
On the cross, Jesus forgave the repentant thief.
On the cross, Jesus forgives us and offers us salvation and eternal life.

How, in carrying my cross, can I offer healing to another?

How, in carrying my cross, can I offer forgiveness to another?

How, in carrying my cross, can I walk with another on his or her journey to God
the Father?

How, in carrying my cross, can I receive healing, forgiveness, and accompaniment on my journey to eternal life?

Twenty-Seven
What's Next

Our days may come to seventy years, or eighty, if our strength endures; yet the best of them are but trouble and sorrow, for they quickly pass, and we fly away. (Psalm 90:10, NIV)

AS A MAN in the age range noted in this Psalm, I find this to be a great passage to sit with and reflect on. There is no need to unwrap a deep hidden meaning: the message is clear. No one knows the span of their life; it may be brief, or it may extend to seventy or eighty years, or maybe even beyond. Most of our years are spent working—working to sustain life, to maintain a certain standard of living, and to be as happy and fruitful as possible until the end. Certainly, we have times of joy and wonderment, but few people are exempt from struggles and pains of one sort or other. Most of our years contain a fair amount of toil and sorrow.

The older a person gets, the quicker each week, month, and year seem to pass. And as each year passes, the more one thinks about one's mortality. Each day draws us closer to an end, and we ask "What's next?" for ourselves and for those we love. Just that process of reflection on the fragility and uncertainty of human life can entail toil and sorrow.

Another passage that for me compliments the one quoted above comes from John's Gospel: "*Very truly I tell you, when you were younger you dressed yourself and went where you wanted; but when you are old you will stretch out your hands, and someone else will dress you and lead you where you do not want to go"* (21:18, NIV).

This passage calls for far more reflection. It can take us beyond the simplicity of the words themselves as we look back on life, and forward in anticipation of what is yet to come.

I see three distinct segments to this passage from John. Let's break it down and begin with *"...when you were younger you dressed yourself and went where you wanted..."*

There is a natural immaturity and even recklessness in all of us when we are young. We are curious and anxious to discover, learn, and enjoy. As the saying goes, "Life is our oyster."

When I was young, pretty much everything was open to me. I did what I wanted, though within fairly tight parameters. As a child, I went about doing what children want to do, often trying to get away with as much as possible. My mind could not yet comprehend the real consequences of anything I did wrong beyond some kind of scolding or punishment.

As I began to "mature," things began to change, but slowly and certainly not an about-face. Yes, I began to understand that my actions could well have consequences for others, yet my prime focus remained on me: what I wanted to do, whom I wanted to hang out with, and in incremental degrees, what path I wanted to pursue for my future.

I wasn't an overly confident kid, and was even less so as an adolescent. Yet I viewed most things as being possible, even if it meant I might have to work harder than others to achieve what I wanted.

The next segment that I want to focus on is *"...when you get older you will stretch out your hands..."*

I mentioned earlier that Joanne and I were young when we married, and young when we had our family. In hindsight, I was not well prepared for the role of either husband or parent, or for the responsibilities that accompany married and family life.

Along each step of the way I have learned (perhaps slowly) whom I was becoming, and the joy and fulfillment—the blessings—of being husband and father. And it happened because our loving Lord listened to our prayers as we reached out asking God's help as a couple, as parents, and as a family.

Together and individually, we stretched out our hands and God gave us the grace, courage, and strength to face and deal with life's struggles and messes. He continues to "grace" us every day.

As an aging seventy-five-year-old, I have had plenty of opportunity to digest both of these brief texts from Sacred Scripture, and even more so throughout this time of the pandemic. Part of the toil and sorrow that seems to walk hand-in-hand with getting older is the fear of physical and/or emotional pain as arthritis sets in, as immunity to disease and viruses decreases, as you begin to realize you cannot do some of the things you used to do, and the things you can still do take a bit longer. There seem to be more appointments; doctors, audiologists, dentists, and optometrists. The pain and sorrow intensify when you see people you love suffer through this process. There is the simple, basic truth that the older we get, the more we need to reach out to others for help, care, support, companionship, and love.

These things can be heavy and a pain to deal with, but they can also be viewed as wonderful opportunities to reflect: on where we have been, on where we have seen and felt the reality of God being with us, on all He has done for us, and all He brought us through as He joined us in our journey. Great comfort, joy, and peace can be found in the so-called little things, the simple things: the laughter of children, new growth in spring, the double rainbow that captures our attention, glistening snow, rabbits hopping around, chipmunks scurrying about with great enthusiasm, even cardinals that seem to respond when you try to mimic their call.

We have the gift of seeing our children succeed in life, watching as they nourish, care for and love their own children. We witness our grandchildren blossom as they mature into young adults with great aspirations and possibilities. How blessed we are to be gifted with this special time—time to observe, time to appreciate.

> Our time is most fruitful when we allow God to take over, to heal those areas of our life that need healing; as we allow God to love us, and to more fully prepare us for that time when we are called home to be in His presence forever.

We also have many opportunities to look ahead and welcome each new day as a gift from God. Our time is most fruitful when we allow God to take over, to heal those areas of our life that need healing; as we allow God to love us, and to more fully prepare us for that time when we are called home to be in His presence forever.

These thoughts and reflections are highlighted more clearly as I look closer at the third and final segment taken from this Gospel passage of John: *"(... you will stretch out your hands, and) someone else will dress you and lead you where you do not want to go."*

It is very disturbing to think of ever being led somewhere you don't want to go, and it stirs up several questions in my mind: Who or what is it that's leading me? Where is it that I don't want to go? Why do I fear going there? What's happening to me and why is this happening, especially now?

Who or what is it that's leading me?

Time may be the driving force that directs where we go. The older we get, the more our time can be filled with the intrusion of many things. However, our time can also be characterized by the absence of many things.

Firstly, as we age, our friends, neighbours, family, and partner also age. Over time, some will have moved away, and some will have died. There is a natural loneliness that accompanies mourning for those who are now absent from your life. That eats away at your time in varying degrees, day by day.

Time becomes an increasing commodity as one gets older. This extra free time can present opportunities for deep reflective thought. Quiet introspection can be positive and very valuable, but it can also lead one down a darker, more negative route, depending on where the thoughts go and the state of one's physical or emotional health.

Older people are not exempt from very real and debilitating struggles. Along with possible physical issues, inner struggles may invade our unfilled time.

Many of us, regardless of age, have over the course of our lives done things and said things in the heat of the moment that we later regret. Or maybe it's the absence of what was done or said that haunts the heart and intrudes and fills the silent moments—things that could have helped someone else feel our compassion, acceptance, care, and love.

I think every human faces some weaknesses of character. Perhaps an addiction to alcohol, drugs, gambling, or any number of things. Or we may have developed certain habits that we no longer even recognize, yet they continue to cause all sorts of harm. Some of the more subtle and damaging habits include gossip, being deceitful, lying or telling only half-truths, or portraying oneself as being better or deserving more than others.

Many if not all families have some issues that have to be faced and dealt with over the years; some may remain an ongoing concern. Memories and thoughts about these can reignite the negative things that have happened, events that were serious enough that they brought dysfunction and harm to relationships that were once believed to be tight, deep, and strengthening. Such reflections can stir up feelings of anger, feelings of guilt, and feelings of regret. How did this happen? What did I do wrong? Why haven't I been able to resolve these issues? Did I do my best to make things right—to make amends? Every day I pray for healing, for a restart, or at least for the grace to accept what is and to be at peace.

I hope the majority of us seniors can look back and reminisce, maybe in awe, at the fullness and richness of our years. Maybe we have memories of years filled with happy, joyful celebratory experiences with family and friends, memories of those we have encountered who have helped us, mentored us, and walked alongside us on our life adventures in both the good and the bad times.

I hope many of us spend time expressing thankfulness for God's presence in our lives, for the many graces received from the Holy Spirit, and for the peace that we feel even as we may struggle with any of the physical limitations that so often are tied to aging. These are just a few examples of what some inner struggles may look like, and some of the real gut-wrenching emotions they stir up.

Now let's look at some of the more physical and emotional toils and sorrows faced by older people.

No matter our religious convictions, I think we all want to go to heaven, to rest in peace whenever our time comes. We may even, if only at times, feel somewhat prepared and ready to meet our God face-to-face. But feeling prepared and ready is quite different from *being* ready right here, right now—we're just not sure we want to go there just yet. In our hearts, we may still have things to resolve, mountains and hills to grade down and level off.

In our minds, we may see and comprehend things in a somewhat unrealistic way. We may have a sense of being lost much of the time, a sense that no one understands, or can be bothered to care. A day or week without getting a call from someone we love might seem like an eternity. So many things can lead us to loneliness we never thought possible, to places we never wanted to go.

In our bodies, we may experience great pain and extreme weariness that can lead us down a long and dark road toward self-medicating on things that are anything but medicinal. Extreme, undaunting pain can drive and direct us toward negative thoughts and decisions. We may begin to indulge in self-pity and begin to question life itself. What's the purpose? Any feeling we have of being "ready" might relate more to a wish to be set free of what seems unbearable than to our desire to share in the joyful presence of the Almighty. We do not want to be led down a road of constant pain and suffering, too tired to go on.

Let me share with you one aspect of my upbringing, my life that provokes in me a strong sense of "someone else dressing me and leading me where I do not want to go."

I was baptized Catholic as an infant. I have tried to practice and live my faith to the best of my ability all my life, and have been an active participant in the sacramental life of the Church for as long as I can remember. I love our Catholic faith, and I love our Catholic Church, with all its rituals and traditions, all that it stands for and all it has to offer. That said, there are many things about our Church—not our faith—that deeply disturb me, to the point of feeling betrayed.

Over time many truths have come to light that reveal great failures within the Church by far too many priests, too many consecrated religious, as well as failures among too many of the faithful laity. I am not referring to simple one-off mistakes but rather to deep, grave failures that have hurt and damaged lives. Reflecting on these failures can slowly eat away at and tear up one's belief system and lead one where one doesn't want to go.

I remember hearing as a child that the Catholic Church was the only true Church through which one could be saved. Relationships with non-Catholics were discouraged, if not outright forbidden.

I remember hearing a story about my father being denied permission to attend the funeral of a non-Catholic neighbour because the service was going to be held in a non-Catholic church. He went anyway because he knew it was the right thing to do.

I have also heard from the pulpit—and more than once—that if you suffer from any mental health issue, you need more faith. That is a denial of reality, but it is more an avoidance of dealing with something not understood. It's a cop-out.

Whether intended or not, the messages heard by people in the pews are not always reflective of what we are told in Sacred Scripture: that all people are God's children (Romans 8:16), brothers and sisters in Christ (Matthew 12:50).

And there is the matter of clergy sexual abuse that has come to the surface over the years. So many people have been abused and betrayed by someone once trusted and held in esteem. What a terrible evil on so many levels. The greater sin may well be in that those instances of abuse were hidden, covered up by the very Church whose responsibility it has always been to bring God's truth to light, God's presence to others. Moving abusive priests from one diocese to another to keep the scandalous truth from the faithful, and the community at large, is never going to bring people to a real knowledge of God: of His tenderness, compassion, and love for all. In these matters, everyone has been betrayed, beginning with the victims, living representatives of Christ Himself.

The Church has been betrayed, along with all who have dedicated their lives to Christ and faithfully lived up to their commitments, to their vows. Priests have been betrayed by brother priests.

All the faithful have been betrayed.

As a deacon I feel hurt, betrayed, and angry over the pain and suffering of so many caused by these abusers. I feel hurt, betrayed and angry at the many bishops who played a role in the denial and cover-up.

I do believe that steps have been taken and measures put in place to address and help end this problem, but that doesn't get the Church off the hook. Those who failed to act promptly and meaningfully have left many, many faithful parishioners frustrated, angry, disappointed, and disillusioned.

We also know of the history of abuse to indigenous children in residential schools here in Canada, the majority of which were operated by the Catholic

Church. It has been known for years, for decades, that many of these children disappeared from those schools. News broadcasts tell us that many parents of the missing children were told their son or daughter had run away. They never returned and were never seen again.

The remains of many children are being found in unmarked burial sites on the grounds of these residential schools and homes. Recently, graves were discovered in British Columbia with indications that over two hundred children were buried, perhaps in one mass grave, on the grounds of one such school. Another site was discovered in Saskatchewan where over seven hundred graves were discovered. Sadly, there will be many more such discoveries over the coming months.

What has happened has been described by many as "genocide," the eradication of the indigenous people, their traditions, their languages, and their lifestyles.

It may take years to fully unravel the truths of why or how such things could happen. Blame and guilt may never be fully determined, but the administration of these schools by the Church raises questions that need to be asked. Residential school survivors tell of the horrendous pain, suffering, and abuse that was inflicted on them as children. One elder who told his story stated, "We used to be a people who had faith, but now we don't."

The misrepresentation of the Church, the abuse in many variations, and the lies and cover-ups have caused many people to lose trust in the clergy. Many have lost trust in the Church, and sadly some have even lost trust in God.

It may sound like I am putting responsibility and blame for these things squarely and solely on the Church. Perhaps I am to some degree, but more so I am recognizing and acknowledging that the Church I have always held dear, defended, and remain committed to is not faultless.

I mentioned before that I was pretty young, just over ten, when I became an altar boy. I was determined to be the best. Mass at that time was celebrated in Latin, not English, and I quickly learned all the responses and the pronunciation of some very tongue-twisting vocabulary. Somehow it all came quite easily, quite naturally to me. It wasn't long before I had the task of helping others learn the role of serving at God's altar, including helping them learn and pronounce the proper Latin responses.

This is the Church in which I found my value as a kid, and as a person. This is the Church through which I discovered the roots of who I am. I learned to know and love God as a child in this Church. It's where I found comfort, solitude, and purpose. Coming to terms with all of these wrongs, committed by people in positions I have long respected, is gut-wrenching at best—an ongoing, painful, and challenging struggle.

We can look at the Church as an institution, or we can see it as a gathering of people wanting to worship and give glory to God. We can identify the Church as the Body of Christ, the living presence of God. The Church established by Christ is the mystery of all of that, united and bound together. St. Paul tells us, *"...you are no longer strangers and foreigners, but you are fellow citizens with the saints and of the household of God, being built on the foundation of the apostles and prophets, Christ Jesus himself being the chief cornerstone"* (Ephesians 2:19–20, WEB).

The institution and the people who gather are subject to human failings and mistakes, but the living presence of God, the vine, is always faithful, always merciful, always welcoming, and inviting us—the branches—to strengthen and stretch out, and to reconnect if we have twisted or bent. The living presence of God is always the truth, and is always redemptive.

Lord, I believe that You are truly and fully present to us
    in Word and in Eucharist.
    I believe that it is You whom I can invite, welcome,
    and physically receive in Holy Communion.
    It is You who desires to enter into me, to reside in my heart,
    to fill me with all the grace and strength to do what You ask,
    to love as You love.

The existence of faith in our lives, and the growth or maturation of faith, demands questions from us. Any real meaningful sense of the presence of the risen Christ, of a loving Father, of the Spirit of light and direction, means that we look at the wonders of creation as well as how society as a whole lives today. How we live our lives affects this world that God created, the world in which we have been placed. We can't do any of that without asking questions.

Some questions need to be asked: what things need to be corrected, and how can we as individuals and as a society help make things better? To come up with any solution or path forward, other questions need to be raised about why and how things went off the rails in the first place. Faith is believing in what we are not able to see or touch, and as such, it should naturally lead to questions, questions that our Abba—Father—wants us to ask.

We know the messiness, the noise, the confusion, and the injustice that go on in the world, in our communities, in our families, and in our lives.

Our challenge as Christians is to hold tight to our belief that despite all we see and witness, God is in charge. We have Jesus' promise that He will never abandon us but will be with us always; that the Holy Spirit will always be present to us to remind us of all Jesus said and did so we might know God's love; that we are His children; that through Christ's passion, death, and resurrection we are heirs to the Kingdom.

It is in our reliance and trust in the love of the Father, the promises of Christ our Saviour, and the grace and guidance of the Spirit that we can see more fully the wonder and awe of life, and all that it holds. There lies our hope, our belief, our conviction that *the best is yet to come*—that in Christ, a *New Day* is here.

...and someone else will dress you and lead you where you do not want to go.

Thought for Reflection:

What is my strongest emotion when I ponder my future?

How do these emotions and feelings align with my relationship with God?

"For I know the plans I have for you," declares the Lord, "plans to prosper you and not to harm you, plans to give you hope and a future." (Jeremiah 29:11, NIV)

Thought for Reflection:

We have no idea what lies ahead for us, what's next.

However, in hindsight we can have an insight into what God may have in mind for us. Looking back, we can have pretty clear pictures of where and when God has walked alongside, holding our hand and leading us forward through circumstances and events we could not have navigated on our own.

Hopefully, our recollections and our moments of looking back have given us cause to trust and rely on God's word, that His plan is that we have hope and a future.

When you think about what might come next for you, and where you go from here, does it fill you with anticipation or anxiety?

Are you hopeful for what God will do in your life, or are you fearful?

Jesus, You are my Lord and my God.
You invite us, You want us to follow You.
You give us Your Word, Your very being
to shine a light on our path of life.
You guide and lead us forward as much as we allow You to.
You help us to follow, to open our hearts
and to surrender our lives to You, for You know what is best for us.
You know what lies ahead.
You know What's Next.

Postscript

IN AN EARLIER chapter, 2020–22: Years of Question, I noted the coronavirus figures as of April 2, 2022: over five hundred million cases and over 6.1 million deaths. Today, December 20, 2022, over 650 million confirmed cases and over 6.6 million deaths have been reported globally.

As I complete this writing, COVID-19 remains a reality, and it continues to ravage and threaten the lives of many people all around the world.

During the course of this pandemic, Ontario, Canada as a whole, and the entire world have gone through periods of lock-down, periods when restrictions were loosened, periods when some were even dropped completely, and periods when they have tightened again. Thus far there have been several variants of COVID; the last two were perhaps less severe and less fatal, but they have proven to be far more contagious.

Today, here at home, almost everything has recently reopened with virtually no restrictions, only the recommendation that we continue to use face masks when in public, and remain vigilant.

Vaccines are approved and immunization shots are well underway, but we are still many months, perhaps years, before enough people will be immunized for this country to be in a position of having control over this virus. The latest strain has resulted in a marked increase in new cases, with hospitalizations increasing daily.

No one wants to go back to lockdown, or any of the more stringent restrictions. We are all tired of this, but that is precisely what many in the medical profession are once again urging us to help keep hospital caseloads at a manageable level.

There is so much uncertainty and anxiety about what may lie ahead, but we are not powerless in the interim; we have a God who listens to our prayers.

Together we plead: *Lord, guide, comfort, and save your people.*

Just before the end of every year, Christians of most denominations enter into the season of Advent, four weeks set aside as a time of expectant waiting for the celebration of the birth of Jesus Christ at Christmas, and in preparation for the second coming of Christ.

While this happens near the end of the calendar year, Advent marks the beginning of the Church year.

It is fitting that I end this exercise as we prepare to say goodbye to 2022 and welcome 2023.

The pandemic still surges and threatens so many lives, and the knowledge of all the pain, fear, and grief that it continues to leave in its path has certainly contributed to this being a long and difficult period for every living being all around the world. It continues to be a very long "Advent," if you will—a time of expectant waiting for the day this fearful contagion is over; for a time when all of us can celebrate the return of some normalcy to life.

For Christians, this is indeed a very long and enduring Advent period: a time of expectant waiting and reflection; a time in which we have an opportunity to allow our saving Lord to change us, to soften our hearts, to more fully prepare us for a much fuller, richer, and greater recognition of the glory of His presence among us.

Our help, our safety, our joy, our trust, and our expectancy in a Happy *New Day* are in the name of the Lord, *Emmanuel,* "God with us."

Epilogue

My Prayer for You

MAY THE WARM inviting rays of Almighty God envelop you
and give you peace.

May the presence, love and healing of our Mighty Saviour
fill every one of your *New Days*
with a heart of gatitude for the life He calls you to.

May the Lord's mighty Spirit grace you
with acceptance of whatever crosses you may carry today,
and with a joyful expectation
may you recognize the awe and wonder
of the workings of the Holy Spirit
as you proceed through life's journey.

May you be filled with an ever-increasing knowledge
of God's infinite and intimate love for you personally,
with an ever-increasing willingness to listen to His voice
in the quiet stillness of your heart,
and to follow His lead
with conviction and surety;

for with God, every day is a *New Day,* a new beginning, a new freshness,
a new opportunity to rejoice and to be glad:
for *you are God's Beloved.*

—Deacon Bob

A Chat with the Father

LORD, THANK YOU for being so very patient with me. I mean, I know you always are, but especially over the last couple of years as you have walked me through this project. It is You who planted the seed, the idea that I write about You—Your presence in my life, in the lives of those around me, and in all creation. You planted the seed, and I resisted so many times.

Father, You stirred something in me whereby I began to wake up a little earlier each morning. I established a routine—I would make a coffee and sit in a favourite chair in our living room. In the quietness and still dim light of early dawn, You made your presence known to me. Perhaps my mind was still dozy, void of distraction and concern, but there in the emptiness, without any activity or deep thought, I felt a calmness. In that stillness, I could hear Your whisper, and it truly is like a gentle breeze that can envelop and stir the soul.

Father, You knew and accepted my difficulty in concentrating, and my reluctance to soak in things or ideas that hadn't been generated by me. I never felt the need to delve deeply into faith, but have always been quite content to simply believe You are with me. I always believed that if it was necessary You would let me know the things I needed to know, the things I needed to change, the direction and way of life You planned for me.

Your leading was made crystal clear the day I proposed to Joanne, the day we were united in the Sacrament of marriage, the day each of our children was born, the arrival of each of our grandchildren, and the day You called me to serve Your people as a deacon.

Father, in these early morning quiet times You brought to my mind many of the events of my life. You have repeatedly shown me over the last couple of years that You are ever-present in the routine of daily life with all its excitement, all its confusion, all its messy blisters and warts; You are also present in times of great peace and joy. You made me aware of how important it is that all of these times be acknowledged, and how every event that happens is worthy of thought and reflection. You made me keenly aware that You have been there through it all, and that You continue to lead me and our family through this precious gift of life.

You have also made me much more aware of just how differently You see me—how You see everyone—than we see ourselves. You know the gifts and talents that You have given to each one of your children—gifts and talents that we so often fail to see in ourselves and fail to develop and exercise to their fullest. You know the graces and strengths that you have placed in our hearts when so often we struggle to see beyond our failings, our weaknesses, and our sins. You see only the infinite goodness and beauty which You instilled in us long before we were born, even while we stumble with our temptations and cringe at all the warts we see when we gaze into the mirror and into our hearts.

Thank You, Father, for the tremendous, unfathomable, unwavering love that You shower upon me, upon all Your creation. Help me; help all of us. Give us the humility to accept, welcome, and receive all that You bestow on us, and in doing so, live our lives in a way that honours You and gives You glory and praise.

Over this time, You have been telling me that the calm and peace that You have given me in these times of quiet reflection is not to be held onto. It's not meant to be private—sharing how I see You even in the clouds of my life just might help others recognize You in their daily lives, amid their own clouds.

Lord, with every recollection, every recognition of You in my life, You were urging me to write it down. Please forgive me, Father, for the many times I hesitated, for the many times I outright rejected the very thought of recording these things.

Thank You, Holy Spirit, for placing in my heart the words to write in those moments when I knew there was something that I was to say but had no words of my own—when I was at a loss. When I allowed my mind to slow down and let You take the lead, that's when words, sentences, and pages flowed from my heart.

This project began, at least in my mind, as an exercise that was somehow meant to help me. As months progressed, I began to realize that it is not so much a matter of me inviting You into my heart, but rather You inviting me into Your presence, into Your heart. That is precisely what You do with me in these still and quiet moments of the early morn: You invite me to spend my day with You in a concrete, peaceful way.

For quite some time You have been nudging me not only to look back on my life and put thoughts and words to paper, but also to share with others the many times and many ways that You have made yourself known to me. Once again, I found myself fighting You. I reasoned how impossible a task that would be. I am, deep down, a private person, and there were simply too many personal matters that I didn't want to share openly. I kept pushing Your urgings out of my mind for well over a year, and it has been a continuing internal fight.

It's time to more deeply and sincerely appreciate Your presence—not only in my life, but in the life of everyone who takes the time and finds that still and quiet space in which they can know and feel You are there with them. Thank you, Father, for the miracle of life, for loving every one of us without bounds or conditions.

This journey has been one continuous conversation with You, Father: a conversation that I want to last forever, a conversation to be shared. I hope that I have listened to and cooperated with Your Holy Spirit throughout this process, as sporadic as it has been, and that this final product will help others see You where You are, walking alongside each one of us, amid the everyday clouds of life. Finally, I hope that it brings You glory.

Conclusion

LIFE AND ALL that it holds, all that it presents to us as joy and challenge and opportunity, has been compared to the experience of riding a rollercoaster. I prefer to think of those ups and downs of life like walking through a maze. There's certainly a sense of venture and challenge as one weaves through various twists and turns, while at the same time stepping over or around obstacles that blur one's sight of the goal: to reach the end, to find the exit.

As human beings, our spiritual life is precisely the same. As we do our best to live our faith, to follow and model ourselves after Jesus, we face many twists and turns, many obstacles that can make us stumble and fall. Our ultimate finish is to be welcomed into God's kingdom. If we are to navigate this course—our adventure of life—with the hope of reaching our final destiny, we need to keep faith, hope, and trust in God.

We often think that if we could only see awesome and wonderful signs, our anxieties, our questions, our doubts and fears would vanish and we would believe more, which would create more faith. The reality is just the reverse: it is faith that creates awe and wonder, and faith that helps us see it.

Faith gives us the hope and conviction that a *New Day* lies ahead and is ready to welcome us in every following minute, hour, or day.

May every minute be the beginning of a *New Day*. May every *New Day* enlighten our minds, uplift our hearts, and bring us into a more intimate relationship with God. And may each *New Day* bring us closer to salvation—to that day when we rejoice in the Presence of the Almighty for all eternity.

With our eyes fixed on the horizon, on the Light of our Lord's promise, and with all the graces He bestows on us, may we dare to conclude our earthly journey with words from Sacred Scripture (2 Timothy, 4:7–8, ASV):

I have fought the good fight,
I have finished the course,
I have kept the faith...

Acknowledgments

FIRST AND FOREMOST, I give thanks to Almighty God for loving every one of us as He does, for revealing Himself to us more and more in the everyday events of life, and for the graces, blessings, and insights freely offered and granted through the Holy Spirit. We simply have to ask in faith.

I am grateful for the times of sitting quietly, listening to our Lord and just soaking in what I was able to as He spoke to my heart. He gave me a sense of warmth through His love, His compassion, and His mercy. That warmth helps me to recognize my brokenness, to see my sins. In that warmth I know God is present, calling me back when I fall, inviting and challenging me to a deeper intimacy with Jesus. He wants me to allow Him to forgive, heal, and welcome me in tenderness.

Thank you, Lord, for the peace and joy that came with the thoughts and words You provided, which otherwise may never have come to the forefront of my mind, let alone found their way to paper.

I am very thankful to Joanne for being my dear wife and friend, for giving me the space and time to write, but even more so for her loving encouragement—not only for this exercise but throughout our fifty-five years of marriage. She has been a true gift to me in my growth as a Catholic Christian, affirming the things I may have done right and pointing out those areas which need attention and more work. I am a better husband, father, and person because of her.

I also express my thanks to all who have been a source of inspiration to me throughout my life, through the example of their faith in God: their patience and their trust that God would indeed hear and answer their prayer in a way, and time, that He knew would be best for them.

I thank our granddaughter for generously consenting to my use of her painting as the cover for this work. Her painting has inspired the title and entire focus of this writing. It is a wonderful depiction of the clouds we all experience on any given day of life, but it also expresses our God-given ability to be stirred and lifted in the expression of hope and expectation of a *New Day*, not only on the horizon but right now in the moment.

I thank another granddaughter for permitting me to share with you her school project which I have included under the heading of "The Journey."

I am very grateful to my wife Joanne, and to Fr. Mickey Prieur, Bridget Corneil, and Richard Corneil, who have read, reviewed, and checked to ensure no personal thought, opinion, or interpretation expressed conflicts with the Catholic faith, and who offered feedback and suggestions where appropriate.

Finally, I thank you who are reading this work, which has been an invitation for my personal growth. I pray that in some small way it may help you in your ongoing spiritual growth as you encounter the presence of God in your every-day life experiences.

May our Loving Lord bless you as you respond to God's call in whichever way He may lead you, and may your response move you to the wonder and awe of every moment when you step forward into God's gift of a *New Day*.

www.ingramcontent.com/pod-product-compliance
Lightning Source LLC
LaVergne TN
LVHW051554080426
835510LV00020B/2971